Critical Thinking through Authentic Video

Expanding Horizons

CEFR
B1-B2

世界を巡る映像で学ぶ総合英語〈中級〉

Charles Browne　田邉祐司

NAN'UN-DO

映像
ストリーミング

ビデオ映像
無料視聴
のご案内

このテキストのビデオ映像を無料で視聴（ストリーミング）できます。
自習用としてご活用ください。
以下のサイトにアクセスしてテキスト番号で検索してください。

https://nanun-do.com　テキスト番号［ **512125** ］

※ 無線 LAN（WiFi）に接続してのご利用を推奨いたします。ストリーミング再生では、動画ファイルは保存されません。再生する度にデータをインターネット経由で読み込みますので、通信量にご注意ください。

※ キャリア回線を使用する場合、お使いのキャリアの料金プラン等によっては、高額なインターネット通信料金が発生する場合がありますのでご注意ください。

※ Expanding Horizons【CEFR B1-B2】映像視聴ページは以下の
QR コードからもご利用になれます。

Foreword

Welcome to Expanding Horizons: Critical Thinking through Authentic Video.

It has long been known that one of the most important factors in developing English language skills over time is regular, daily exposure to input in English that is both at an appropriate level, as well as of personal interest to the learner. Expanding Horizons: Critical Thinking through Authentic Video is a 4-skill book that is designed to help you improve your English skills through exposure to authentic, award-winning videos that are carefully graded to follow the CEFR framework. The first four units have videos, texts and activities that are at the B1 level, the next six units are at the B1+ level, and the final four units are at the B2 level.

Although input is an essential starting point for language learning, it is not enough – regular, daily output, too, is crucial if you want to be able to advance beyond the beginner level. Expanding Horizons addresses this by taking a strong student-centered approach, which gives lots of opportunities for you to discuss and share your ideas, experiences and opinions with other students in English, using language in ways that will encourages the development of critical thinking skills. We have tried to strike a balance between fluency-oriented writing and pair/group activities (meaning you don't have to worry about making mistakes in English), and accuracy-focused shadowing, dictation/dictogloss and vocabulary development activities that will help improve your pronunciation, listening and speaking skills.

We believe that English language learning materials as well as the learning experience itself should be interesting, easy and fun and have done our best to make Expanding Horizons exactly that. We hope that you will enjoy studying English with this book and that it will help you to expand your horizons!

Dr. Charles Browne
Dr. Yuji Tanabe

Introduction to Activities in a Typical Unit:

1. **WARM UP: Talk about it**
   This activity is picture-based and designed to activate your real-world knowledge on the topic of the unit.

2. **VOCABULARY: Matching**
   This activity teaches the most important vocabulary words needed to understand the contents of the video. Definitions are given in easy English and match the meanings given in the video

3. **Pushed Output Writing**
   This simple but challenging activity asks you to write original sentences in English using the new words you've just learned. Research shows this is a great way to help process the meaning of a word and to remember it longer.

4. **VIDEO: Before Watching**
   This activity usually asks you to make some predictions about what you think the video might be about. It helps draw you into the video as well as activate your knowledge on the topic.

5. **VIDEO: While Watching**
   There are several types of activities in this section, all of which can be characterized as "while-listening" activities, designed to help you to listen more actively and comprehend the video more fully.

6. **VIDEO: After Watching**
   These are a wide range of activities in this section, all of which use the content and ideas from the videos as a jumping point into more student-centered, speaking activities that help to personalize the lesson.

7. **DISCUSSION**
   This is a student-centered speaking activity designed to help you to think more deeply about the video, and to begin to communicate and share your ideas and opinions with others about this topic.

8. **WRITING: Critical Thinking**

This activity is designed to help you to think more deeply about the topic as well as to move from an input-focus (the video and readings) to a more output-focus. This is done by asking you to write your ideas on the topic, which will also help you with the speaking activities later in the unit.

9. **QUOTABLE QUOTES**

This picture-based activity introduces a quote, usually from a famous person, that is related to the topic of the unit. It is designed to help you to think deeply about the topic you have been studying.

10. **VOICE DICTION: Video Shadowing**

The dictation part of this activity gives you practice in developing your intensive listening skills while the shadowing part of the activity helps you to work on and improve your pronunciation, especially at the sentence level.

11. **CRITICAL DISCUSSION**

This activity builds on the writing activity given earlier in the unit, providing you with a real audience for your writing as well as a chance to discuss and think more critically about the topic at hand.

12. **Vocabulary: Split-Crossword Active Review**

This is a pair work activity designed not only to help you review the words in this unit but also to build the very real-world communication strategy of being able to describe words you don't know.

13. **OPTIONAL PROJECTS: Individual and Group**

Each unit provides an optional projects should you want to extend the lesson or dig more deeply into the topic. Often the projects culminate with presenting the results to the class in the form of a PowerPoint, a poster or some kind of presentation, while encouraging the audience to actively ask follow-up questions.

Contents

Unit 1
5 Things You Can't Buy on High Street <Shopping>

Learning Goals	Vocabulary from the Video
Speaking Skills: ● **guessing** Writing Skills: ● **classified ads**	Words related to personal belongings Words for describing objects

WARM UP: Talk about it

Work with a partner and answer the questions below.

1. Have you ever bought something that was not new? What was it?
2. Have you ever been to a second-hand shop? Did you see any unusual or interesting things? Did you buy anything?

VOCABULARY: Matching

Match the words and phrases (1-8) and their definitions (a-h).

1. vintage	____	a. a band worn around the head
2. cape	____	b. one of the many light, soft things on a bird's body
3. feather	____	c. strange or unusual
4. headband	____	d. used, not new
5. knight in armor	____	e. an old item of high quality
6. second-hand	____	f. a servant of the king in a protective metal suit
7. weird	____	g. a short, sleeveless cloak
8. magical	____	h. especially enjoyable

Pushed Output Writing

Now try to write an original sentence using each of the words above.

1. vintage ______________________________

2. cape ______________________________

3. feather ______________________________

4. headband ______________________________

5. knight in armor ______________________________

6. second-hand ______________________________

7. weird ______________________________

8. magical ______________________________

VIDEO: Before Watching

Think about the main shopping street in your town or city. What kinds of things can you buy there? Make a list.

______________________ ______________________

______________________ ______________________

______________________ ______________________

______________________ ______________________

______________________ ______________________

VIDEO: While Watching

Activity 1:

Look at the picture from the video. What unusual things do you think Sarah finds? Watch the video and write the five items.

1. ______________________
2. ______________________
3. ______________________
4. ______________________
5. ______________________

Activity 2:

Watch the video again. Read the sentences and circle the correct words.

1. Sarah is looking for (everyday items/unusual objects).
2. The cape Sarah tries on is probably (handmade/magic).
3. You can find things like (capes and hats/sunglasses and headbands) in High street shops.
4. One of the strangest things Sarah found in the shop was (a knight in armor/a castle).
5. The video says that a gramophone is something we (use/don't use) nowadays.
6. The rings are special because they are also (boxes/watches).
7. The drawings of animals are more than (75/175) years old.

VIDEO: After Watching

SPEAKING

Look at the picture in Activity 1 again. Choose something in the picture but don't tell your partner. Ask and answer questions to guess your partner's item.

Below is some language to help you.

Is it made of wood?

No, it isn't.

Is it very old?

Yes, it is.

Can you wear it?

No, you can't.

Is it this statue?

Yes, it is.

DISCUSSION

Work in groups. Discuss the topics below.

- Why do you think used shops are so popular?
- If you were to run a used shop as a business, what kind of items would you focus on? Why?

Now choose someone as spokesperson for your group. Present the key points of your discussion to the class.

WRITING: Critical Thinking

Do you buy and sell things online? Do you know any apps or websites that help you do this? Read the advertisement below. Would you buy this item?

Now think of an item you would like to sell. Write an advertisement (ad) for the website.

- Write a heading for your ad including the price.
- Describe the item in detail.
- List its selling points.
- Point out any defects it may have.

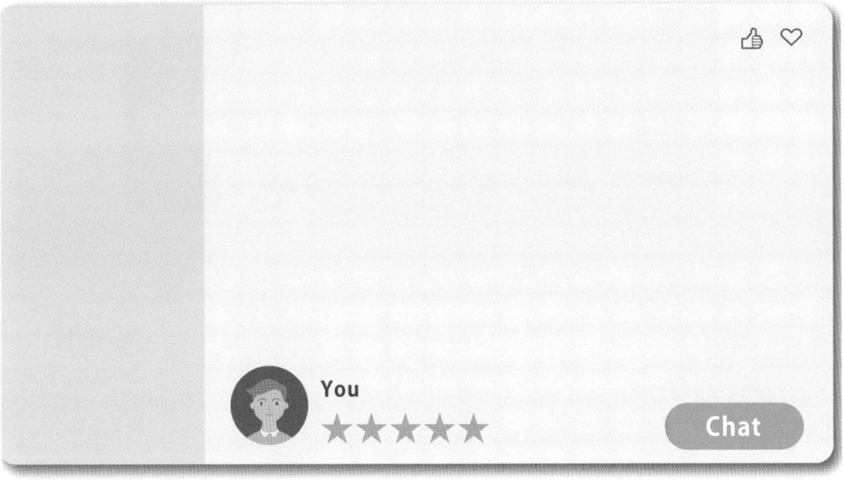

QUOTABLE QUOTES:

"Style is the only thing you can't buy. It's not in a shopping bag, a label, or a price tag. It's something reflected from our soul to the outside world—an emotion."

*By Alber Elbaz**

*Alber Elbaz (1961~2021) Israeli fashion designer

Look at the quote above. Think about this unit. What do you think the quote means?

VOICE DICTION: Video Shadowing

1. Start the video at 2:37 and play. Fill in the blank with the missing words.
   "These animal (   ) are over (   ) years old!"
2. Watch the scene and pronounce at the same time. Repeat several times until you can do it smoothly.

CRITICAL DISCUSSION

Make groups of 3-4 students. Read each ad one by one. Then …

- Choose the ad(s) with the most interesting ideas.
- Prepare to present those to the class in English, explaining why you thought they were the most interesting.

VOCABULARY: Split-Crossword Active Review

Work in pairs.
Each of you has half of today's key words. Ask and give hints in English without saying the word and try to complete the puzzle. See the example below.

A: Excuse me, what is 4 down?
B: Oh, it's a thing you drink from.
A: Do you mean "glass"?
B: Yes, that's right! What is 2 across?...

Example:

Student A

Student B

Now, student A, turn to page **121** and student B, turn to page **128** and try to complete the puzzle using only English.

Optional CLIL Project: A Sustainable Wardrobe

*CLIL: Content and Language Integrated Learning

In this project, you will explore the importance of reducing consumerism* and reusing items in the fight against the climate emergency.

*consumerism : The theory that an increasing consumption of goods is good is for economy.

1) Work in small groups and discuss how often you buy new clothes, shoes and other tangible* products. Then talk about if you ever buy these things second-hand, from shops like the one in the video or markets.

   *tangible : if something is tangible, you can touch or feel it.

2) Look online for data that shows that the fashion industry can be terribly damaging to the planet due to the water pollution it causes, water consumption, waste, as well as many other ethical issues.

3) Research to find out more about the problems with fast fashion and try to come up with practical solutions. Discuss think about what you can do on a personal and local level.

One idea could be to set up a swap shop where everyone brings in items of clothing, books, etc that they no longer want and exchange them with other students. You could write up a description of the items you bring in or give an oral presentation.

Another idea is to "upcycle" old clothes or belongings into new items, for example, an old sweater can easily be turned into a scarf and hat. You could search for ideas online and share with or demonstrate for the class.

CEFR GOALS SELF- EVALUATION	
I can use English to make guesses about things.	1---2---3---4---5
I can write a simple advertizement.	1---2---3---4---5
I can understand words related to personal belongings.	1---2---3---4---5
I can understand and use words for describing objects.	1---2---3---4---5

Unit 2
High Tech High School
<School>

Learning Goals	Vocabulary from the Video
Speaking Skills: • **interviewing** Writing Skills: • **Writing FAQs***	Words related to education Phrasal verbs

*FAQs Frequently Asked Questions

WARM UP: Talk about it

Work with a partner and answer the questions below.

1. What kind of technology was used at your high school?
2. Did it make learning more interesting? Explain.

VOCABULARY: Matching

Match the words and phrases (1-8) and their definitions (a-h).

1. project work	____	a. to make something
2. term	____	b. a public display of art or items of interest
3. exhibition	____	c. to discover a fact or piece of information
4. produce	____	d. to examine something in detail to learn about it
5. join in	____	e. a time period of the academic school year
6. give up	____	f. to stop making an effort, to admit defeat
7. find out	____	g. to do an activity with people
8. explore	____	h. work focused on completing a specific task

Pushed Output Writing

Now try to write an original sentence using each of the words above.

1. project work ______________________________
____

2. term ______________________________
____

3. exhibition ______________________________
____

4. produce ______________________________
____

5. join in ______________________________
____

6. give up ______________________________
____

7. find out ______________________________
____

8. explore ______________________________
____

VIDEO: Before Watching

1. Watch the introduction of the video up to 0:16. Write down the key words you hear.

2. Think about these things in your own school. Discuss your ideas with your partner. Then share with the class.

VIDEO: While Watching

Activity 1:

Watch the video. Write down one thing you like about High Tech High School and one thing you don't like.

Now compare your ideas with a partner.

Activity 2:

Watch the video again. Read the sentences about High Tech High School and circle T (true) or F (false). Correct the false sentences.

1	**The teachers are only there to help guide the students.**	**T**	**F**
2	**The teachers give each group of students a project to do.**	**T**	**F**
3	**The play is about things the students have already learned.**	**T**	**F**
4	**The students will present their projects at an exhibition.**	**T**	**F**
5	**The students are worried that they won't finish their projects on time.**	**T**	**F**
6	**Not many people go to see the exhibition.**	**T**	**F**
7	**Students pass or fail, depending on their work for the exhibition.**	**T**	**F**
8	**Brian can't solve the problem with his machine.**	**T**	**F**

VIDEO: After Watching

SPEAKING

You are going to interview Brian. Write 5 questions to him.

1. ____________________
____
2. ____________________
____
3. ____________________
____
4. ____________________
____
5. ____________________
____

With a partner, take turns to imagine you are Brian or the interviewer. Ask your questions and answer your partner's questions.

DISCUSSION

Work in groups. Discuss the topic below.

Education in Japan is mostly teacher-centered, with the teachers speaking most of the time and students just silently taking notes and memorizing what the teacher says. High Tech High School seems to take almost the opposite approach. Discuss the strengths and weaknesses of each approach. Which do you think is the better way to learn? Why?

Now choose someone as spokesperson for your group. Present the key points of your discussion to the class.

WRITING: Critical Thinking

1. Look at the FAQs of a school website.

https://www.greenhillshighschool.com/

Green Hills High School

Q: How can I join the school?

A: ***To enrol fot the next school year, you'll need to fill in an admissions from and hand it in at the school reception desk.***

Q: How many students are there in each class?

A: ***The average number of students per class is 18 in Years 7 to 11. There are approximately 12 students per class in Years 12 and 13, depending on the subject.***

Q: Are students expected to do homework?

A: ***Yes. Not all learning takes place at school so it is important that students spend some time doing homework or working on projects after school.***

2. With your group, write questions for the FAQ section of the High Tech High School website. Then write answers for three of the questions on the website below.

https://www.greenhillshighschool.com/

High Tech High School

Q:

A:

Q:

A:

Q:

A:

QUOTABLE QUOTES:

"Teachers open the door, but you must enter by yourself."

— *Chinese Proverb*

Look at the quote above. Think about this unit. What do you think the quote means?

VOICE DICTION: Video Shadowing

1. Start the video at 0:31 and play. Fill in the blank with the missing words.
   "This is (   ) in California, a totally new (   ) school."
2. Watch the scene and pronounce at the same time. Repeat several times until you can do it smoothly.

CRITICAL DISCUSSION

Make groups of 3-4 students. Read each FAQ one by one. Then ...

- Choose the FAQs with the most interesting ideas.
- Prepare to present those to the class in English, explaining why you thought they were the most interesting.

VOCABULARY: Split-Crossword Active Review

Work in pairs.
Each of you has half of today's key words. Ask and give hints in English without saying the word and try to complete the puzzle. See the example below.

A: Excuse me, what is 4 down?
B: Oh, it's a thing you drink from.
A: Do you mean "glass"?
B: Yes, that's right! What is 2 across?...

Example:

Student A

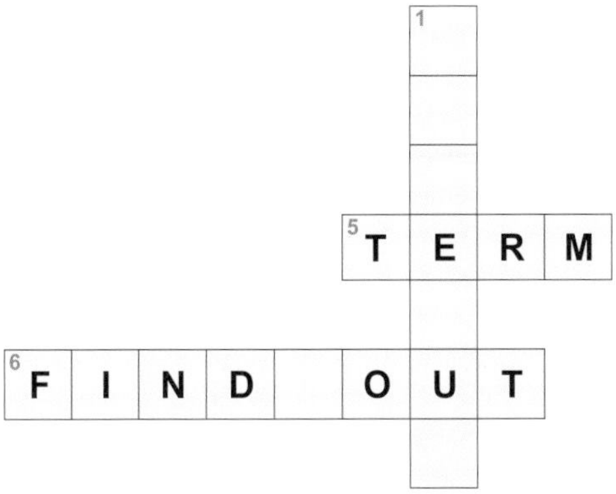

Student B

Now, student A, turn to page **121** and student B, turn to page **128** and try to complete the puzzle using only English.

Optional CLIL Project: Innovative Schools Competition

Goal: to design a poster presentation about an imaginary school.

Work in groups. Imagine you go to a school that is very different from your own school. Your school has just entered a competition to find the most innovative school in Japan. The winning school will be featured in a TV documentary.

Work together and make a poster to present to the class that explains how your school is innovative and why it should win the competition. You can choose some of the following areas to cover in your poster.

- subjects
- facilities
- teachers
- motto/philosophy
- timetable
- evaluation

Please also come up with a name for your school. As a group, discuss the main ideas for your school. Then divide the work up and each learner can write about one of the areas. When you have all the information you need, make a poster to present the key information.

Finally, groups present their posters to the class. End by voting on the most innovative school.

CEFR GOALS SELF- EVALUATION	
I can use English to interview people.	1---2---3---4---5
I can write a simple FAQ statement.	1---2---3---4---5
I can understand words related to education.	1---2---3---4---5
I can understand and use phrasal verbs.	1---2---3---4---5

Unit 3

Plogging
<Environment>

Learning Goals	Vocabulary from the Video
Speaking Skills: ● **conversation** Writing Skills: ● **emails**	Words related to fitness Words related to the environment

WARM UP: Talk about it

Work with a partner and answer the questions below.

1. Do you like running or any other kind of exercise? Why?
2. Do you ever do anything at the same time as exercising (for example, listening to music)? Share as many ideas as you can think of.

VOCABULARY: Matching

Match the words and phrases (1-8) and their definitions (a-h).

1. fitness	____	a. the things in your house which you throw away
2. jogging	____	b. to make your body stronger
3. get fit	____	c. powerful, positive excitement and interest
4. clean up	____	d. the act of doing a slow, steady run
5. food packaging	____	e. to wash or clean something
6. rubbish	____	f. good physical condition
7. passion	____	g. the thing used to close off and protect food from damage
8. household waste	____	h. another word for trash, the things you throw away

Pushed Output Writing

Now try to write an original sentence using each of the words above.

1. fitness ______________________________
____
2. jogging ______________________________
____
3. get fit ______________________________
____
4. clean up ______________________________
____
5. food packaging ______________________________
____
6. rubbish ______________________________
____
7. passion ______________________________
____
8. household waste ______________________________
____

VIDEO: Before Watching

In groups discuss what environmental problems you have in your town and then rank them in order of seriousness.

1. ____________________
2. ____________________
3. ____________________
4. ____________________
5. ____________________

VIDEO: While Watching

Activity 1:

Watch the video and answer the questions below.

1. What two words is "plogging" made from?

   ____

   ____

2. Define both words

   ____

   ____

3. Why did the organizers start plogging?

   ____

   ____

Activity 2:

Watch the video again and complete the gaps with a single word.

1. Dermot and I decided to start plogolution because back in 2018 we went for a run together and came across a lot of ____________.
2. We welcome everyone, all sorts of ____________ abilities, from your slow walkers to your really fast runners.
3. They have to ____________ together to make sure they don't miss any litter and they find a lot more than you might imagine!
4. Old food packaging, ____________ waste... The whole plogging team are shocked by the amount of rubbish they find.
5. It's a great chance for the younger team members to learn about how to look after the ____________ and how they can help in their community.

VIDEO: After Watching

SPEAKING

Answer the following questions in small groups:

1. What are the benefits of plogging?
2. Do you think plogging is a good idea? Why or why not?
3. Would plogging be popular in your hometown?
4. Where could you go plogging in your hometown?
5. What other things can you do to help the environment?

DISCUSSION

Work in groups.

Pick one of the questions in the previous section and discuss it further, adding more details and support for your ideas so that you can present to the class.

Now choose someone as spokesperson for your group. Present the key points of your discussion to the class.

WRITING: Critical Thinking

Imagine you are going to set up a plogging club at your school. Now write an email newsletter to the rest of the students at the school explaining what plogging is, why it's a good idea, where and when it will take place and what people should bring.

The email newsletter should have a subject line, a clear opening paragraph introducing plogging and finally, include an invitation to join the class on a plogging trip.

New mail

For

Subject

SEND

QUOTABLE QUOTES:

"The ultimate test of a moral society is the kind of world that it leaves to its children."

*By Dietrich Bonhoeffer**

*Dietrich Bonhoeffer (1906~1945) German Protestant theologian

Look at the quote above. Think about this unit. What do you think the quote means?

VOICE DICTION: Video Shadowing

1. Start the video at 0:47 and play. Fill in the blank with the missing words.
   "Dermot and I decided to start plogolution because (   ) we went for a run together and came across (   ) rubbish."
2. Watch the scene and pronounce at the same time. Repeat several times until you can do it smoothly.

CRITICAL DISCUSSION

Make groups of 3-4 students. Read each email one by one. Then....

- Choose the emails with the most interesting ideas.
- Prepare to present those to the class in English, explaining why you thought they were the most interesting.

VOCABULARY: Split-Crossword Active Review

Work in pairs.
Each of you has half of today's key words. Ask and give hints in English without saying the word and try to complete the puzzle. See the example below.

A: Excuse me, what is 4 down?
B: Oh, it's a thing you drink from.
A: Do you mean "glass"?
B: Yes, that's right! What is 2 across? ...

Example:

Student A

Student B

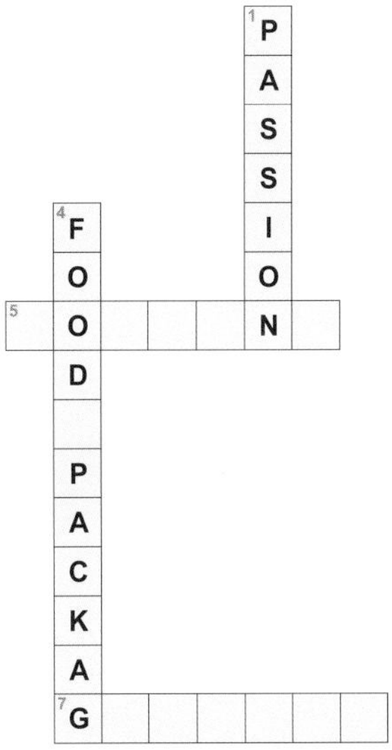

Now, student A, turn to page **122** and student B, turn to page **129** and try to complete the puzzle using only English.

Optional CLIL Project: Let's go plogging!

Work in small groups and plan a day out plogging. In your group decide:

- Where in the city you are going to plog
- How long you are going to plog for
- What your objectives are
- How you are going to get there
- What equipment you are going to need
- What you are going to do with the rubbish afterwards
- How you are going to encourage other people to get involved

After planning the activity in groups, present your ideas to the rest of the class. Then vote on the best plan and, if you are enthusiastic, go plogging as a class!

CEFR GOALS SELF- EVALUATION	
I can talk about plogging with others.	1---2---3---4---5
I can write an email.	1---2---3---4---5
I can understand words related to fitness.	1---2---3---4---5
I can understand words related to the environment.	1---2---3---4---5

Unit 4
Debate Challenge <Education>

Learning Goals	Vocabulary from the Video
Speaking Skills: • **debate** Writing Skills: • **essay**	Words related to education Words related to politics

WARM UP: Talk about it

Work with a partner and answer the questions below.

1. Have you ever watched a school debate or seen one on the Internet? What did you think?
2. What do you think would be the most important skills for a good debater to have? Can you think of any jobs good debaters might get?

VOCABULARY: Matching

Match the words and phrases (1-8) and their definitions (a-h).

1. compete against	____	a. a place where children from different communities learn together
2. election	____	b. a person between the age of 13 and 19 years of age
3. argument	____	c. a formal public discussion on a topic of interest
4. society	____	d. a system and group of people that rule a nation
5. teenager	____	e. the process of choosing someone by voting
6. mixed school	____	f. to try to beat others at something
7. government	____	g. a group of people living together in an orderly way
8. debate	____	h. a discussion in which you disagree with someone

Pushed Output Writing

Now try to write an original sentence using each of the words above.

1. compete against ______________________________

____

2. election ______________________________

____

3. argument ______________________________

____

4. society ______________________________

____

5. teenager ______________________________

____

6. mixed school ______________________________

____

7. government ______________________________

____

8. debate ______________________________

____

VIDEO: Before Watching

1. Should children be able to vote in an election at the age of 14? Why or why not? Discuss in pairs.

2. Share your ideas as a class. Take a final vote.

VIDEO: While Watching

Activity 1:

Watch the video. Answer the questions with one of the names below.

ERIN MELANIE CHELSEA

1. Who has strong opinions but sometimes can get a bit too angry?

____

2. Who has good ideas but can be a nervous speaker?

____

3. Who wants to study law at university?

____

Activity 2:

Watch the video again. Read the sentences and circle T (true) or F (false). Correct the false sentences.

1	The children have never done debates before.	T	F
2	Chelsea doesn't like speaking to an audience.	T	F
3	Kingsford school think children should be allowed to vote at 14.	T	F
4	Chelsea thinks children should focus on exams not politics.	T	F
5	Erin feels ready to vote.	T	F
6	Melanie thinks children don't know enough about politics to vote.	T	F
7	The children have learned a lot from the competition.	T	F

VIDEO: After Watching

Natural Speech

1. Watch the video of the final debate again and read the quotes below.
   - "As teenagers, we have exams to worry about, we have school life to worry about. Why should we feel that we should be forced to be adults? Let us enjoy our teenager life!"
   - "Society has moved on, young teenagers are taking on more adult activities, why should voting not be included?"
   - "I'm 14 and I don't feel ready to vote. We don't go to school to learn about politics, we go to school to learn about English, Maths, Science; key skills that we need in everyday life."
   - "But voting is not hard. You choose a party you like, and you vote. I am a 14 year-old and I am a citizen of the United Kingdom and we have the right to decide our fate and future."
   - "You said that voting isn't hard. You pick a party that you like, and you vote. That shows that actually children our age don't know anything about politics because I think that it's much more than that!"
2. Discuss in pairs. Who do you think delivers the best argument? Why?

DISCUSSION

Work in groups.

Choose one of the debate topics below.

- Boys and girls should go to separate schools.
- Children should have to wear a school uniform.
- Homework is a waste of time.

Divide yourselves into two teams:

Team 1: Write 5 arguments in favor.

Team 2: Write 5 arguments against.

1. ______________________________

   ____

2. ______________________________

   ____

3. ______________________________

   ____

4. ______________________________

   ____

5. ______________________________

   ____

Debate with the other team:

In our opinion, it's better to wear a uniform so everyone looks the same.

We disagree. It's more important to show your individual style.

WRITING: Critical Thinking

1. Organize the linking words below in the correct columns. Add any more that you know.

However	Firstly	To sum up	Secondly
Also	In conclusion	In addition	But

Introducing	Addition	Contrast	Concluding

2. Now, write an essay about your debate topic. Explain both sides of the argument and give your own opinion. Try to use the phrases from the previous activity.

QUOTABLE QUOTES:

"It is better to debate a question without settling it than to settle a question without debating it."

*By Joseph Joubert**

* Joseph Joubert (1754~1824) French moralist and essayist

Look at the quote above. Think about this unit. What do you think the quote means?

VOICE DICTION: Video Shadowing

1. Start the video at 2:37 and play. Fill in the blank with the missing words

   "You pick (   ) that you like, and you (   )."

2. Watch the scene and pronounce at the same time. Repeat several times until you can do it smoothly.

CRITICAL DISCUSSION

Make groups of 3-4 students. Read each essay one by one. Then ...

- Choose the essay(s) with the most interesting ideas.
- Prepare to present those to the class in English, explaining why you thought they were the most interesting.

VOCABULARY: Split-Crossword Active Review

Work in pairs.
Each of you has half of today's key words. Ask and give hints in English without saying the word and try to complete the puzzle. See the example below.

A: Excuse me, what is 4 down?
B: Oh, it's a thing you drink from.
A: Do you mean "glass"?
B: Yes, that's right! What is 2 across? ...

Example:

Student A

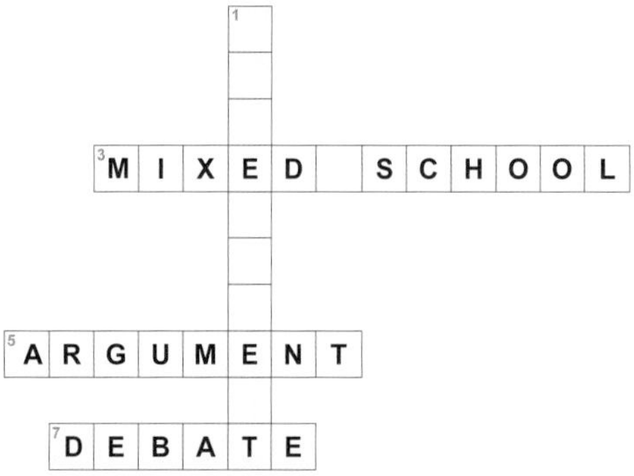

Student B

Now, student A, turn to page **122** and student B, turn to page **129** and try to complete the puzzle using only English.

Optional CLIL Project: The Right to Vote

In pairs, learners write a historical fact file about the voting system in Japan.
Your fact file should include:

- a timeline of important dates in the history of their country
- when voting started
- when women were given the right to vote
- what is the current voting age
- how often there is an election
- a profile of an important person in the history of voting in Japan- what they did and why it was important to their voting system

Pairs then present their fact files to the rest of the class.

CEFR GOALS SELF- EVALUATION	
I can debate about topics related to school.	1---2---3---4---5
I can argue a point of view.	1---2---3---4---5
I can understand words related to education.	1---2---3---4---5
I can understand and use words related to politics.	1---2---3---4---5

Unit 5

The Real Story of Tutankhamun

<History>

Learning Goals	Vocabulary from the Video
Speaking Skills: • **Discussion** Writing Skills: • **Newspaper reports**	Words related to stories & legends Words related to health

WARM UP: Talk about it

Work with a partner and answer the questions below.

1. Have you ever been to a museum? Which ones?
2. When you looked at the objects, did you ever try to imagine what people lived like long ago? Give examples.

VOCABULARY: Matching

Match the words and phrases (1-8) and their definitions (a-h).

1. resting place	____	a.	examining a dead body to find the cause of death
2. tomb	____	b.	a doctor who uses X-rays to help patients
3. ancient	____	c.	something that is very valuable
4. treasure	____	d.	something that very old
5. limp	____	e.	a photo taken with electromagnetic radiation
6. radiologist	____	f.	a small building or stone box where a dead body is put
7. autopsy	____	g.	a politer way of saying tomb or grave
8. x-ray	____	h.	to walk in a slow or awkward way due to injury

Pushed Output Writing

Now try to write an original sentence using each of the words above.

1. resting place ____________________

2. tomb ____________________

3. ruler ____________________

4. treasure ____________________

5. ancient ____________________

6. radiologist ____________________

7. autopsy ____________________

8. x-ray ____________________

VIDEO: Before Watching

Work with a partner. What do you know about ancient Egypt? What questions do you have?

I know...	I want to know...

VIDEO: While Watching

Activity 1:

Put the events below in the order that they appear in the video. Write the numbers (1-4) in the blank to the left.

____ a. Dallas Campbell rides a chariot.

____ b. Dallas Campbell finds objects in the tomb which prove his ideas.

____ c. Dallas Campbell sees pieces of several chariots in a tomb.

____ d. Dallas Campbell finds out something interesting about Tutankhamun's body.

Activity 2:

Watch again. Read and complete Dallas Campbell's notes.

14th SEPTEMBER

This morning I visited the Valley of the (1) ______________, where many ancient Egyptian rulers are buried.

As I was exploring the tomb of Tutankhamun, I noticed how (2) ______________ it was.

Another thing that surprised me was that the paintings on the walls were so (3) ______________ and simple.

This shows that Tutankhamun died unexpectedly. We've discovered that he was only (4) ______________ years old when he died.

Later, I met Professor Salim who took an x-ray of Tutankhamun's remains and we discovered that he had a problem with his (5) ______________.

We believe that it was custom in ancient Egypt to be buried with (6) ______________, since we don't think the young king was able to ride one.

Because of his foot, it's likely that (7) ______________ was very difficult and painful for Tutankhamun.

VIDEO: After Watching

SPEAKING

1. Tutankhamun was buried with objects that were important to, or represented him. Choose five objects that you think represent your life.

   1. ______________________
   2. ______________________
   3. ______________________
   4. ______________________
   5. ______________________

2. Now show your group. Ask and answer questions.

DISCUSSION

King Tut was a child king. Imagine you are ten years old. As king/queen, you are the ruler of your country. You want your country to be a wonderful place for children. In small groups, write down the things important to children. Decide what to do about the things you wrote down.

Now choose someone as spokesperson for your group. Present the key points of your discussion to the class.

WRITING: Critical Thinking

1. You are a journalist. Plan a newspaper report about Dallas Campbell's findings. Use the transcript and make notes about the information you can include.

   Notes:

2. Now write your newspaper report. Remember to include:
   - a headline
   - a topic sentence that explains what the report is about
   - facts about what Campbell discovered (in chronological order)

QUOTABLE QUOTES:

"A generation which ignores history has no past and no future."

*By Robert A. Heinlein**

*Robert A. Heinlein (1907~1988) American science fiction writer

Look at the quote above. Think about this unit. What do you think the quote means?

VOICE DICTION: Video Shadowing

1. Watch again from 02:15 to 02:20. What does Dallas say? Complete the sentence.

   "I can't do it with two legs, (   ) one leg!"

2. Look at these additional examples. When do you think we use the underlined phrase?

   a. I can barely jog for five minutes, <u>let alone</u> run a marathon.

   b. I haven't saved enough money for a bike, <u>let alone</u> a car.

   c. The baby can't even sit up yet, <u>let alone</u> walk.

   d. Many children have never even seen snow, <u>let alone</u> build a snowman.

   e. I haven't even been abroad, <u>let alone</u> travel around the world.

CRITICAL DISCUSSION

Make groups of 3-4 students. Read each interview one by one. Then …

- Choose the interviews with the most interesting ideas.
- Prepare to present those to the class in English, explaining why you thought they were the most interesting.

VOCABULARY: Split-Crossword Active Review

Work in pairs.
Each of you has half of today's key words. Ask and give hints in English without saying the word and try to complete the puzzle. See the example below.

A: Excuse me, what is 4 down?
B: Oh, it's a thing you drink from.
A: Do you mean “glass”?
B: Yes, that's right! What is 2 across? ...

Example:

Student A

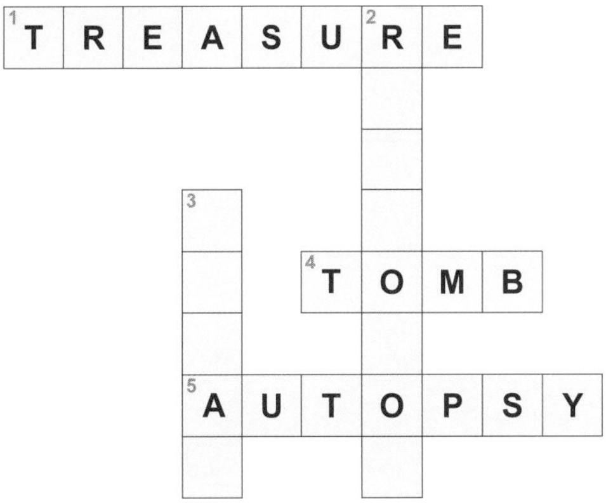

Student B

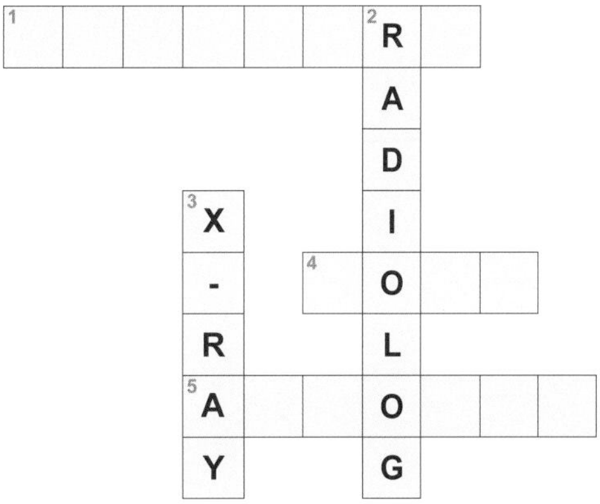

Now, student A, turn to page **123** and student B, turn to page **130** and try to complete the puzzle using only English.

Optional CLIL Project: Removing barriers

As you learned in the video, King Tutankhamun had a physical disability which made it very difficult for him to walk. As a king, he likely had people to help him. In your group, try to imagine what problems he might have come up against while moving around the city.

In your group, discuss what barriers there are in your town (or school) for people with disabilities, for example, wheelchair users, people who have difficulty walking and people with visual impairments. After discussion, choose one disability to focus on. Then analyze how accessible your town center or school is, making a note of any potential problems.

Finally, write up a report and prepare a presentation of your findings.
Try to draw up designs of any improvements that could be made and present these to the class.

CEFR GOALS SELF- EVALUATION	
I can have discussions about history with others.	1---2---3---4---5
I can write a newspaper report.	1---2---3---4---5
I can understand words related to stories and legends.	1---2---3---4---5
I can understand words related to health.	1---2---3---4---5

Unit 6

Saving the Flying Rivers <Environment>

Learning Goals	Vocabulary from the Video
Speaking Skills: • **debate** Writing Skills: • **writing a report**	Words related to the environment Words related to science

WARM UP: Talk about it

Work with a partner and try to answer the questions below. Use the internet to check your answers.

1. Where is the Amazon River?
2. What types of animals live there?
3. How long is it?
4. Why is it special?

VOCABULARY: Matching

Match the words and phrases (1-8) and their definitions (a-h).

1. atmosphere	____	a. ability to understand what is important in life
2. pump	____	b. something that is very beautiful
3. breathtaking	____	c. to make water move using a machine
4. perspective	____	d. the air around us
5. threatened	____	e. to change from a liquid into a gas
6. replant	____	f. the process by which a plant gives off
7. evaporate	____	g. something that is at risk of harm
8. transpiration	____	h. water to move a plant or tree to a new location

Pushed Output Writing

Now try to write an original sentence using each of the words above.

1. atmosphere ______________________________

2. pump ______________________________

3. breathtaking ______________________________

4. perspective ______________________________

5. threatened ______________________________

6. replant ______________________________

7. evaporate ______________________________

8. transpiration ______________________________

VIDEO: Before Watching

Work in pairs. Which of these sentences do you think are true?

- 80% of the Earth's original forests have been cleared or destroyed.
- Trees are the longest living organisms on Earth, and never die of old age.
- A large tree can 'drink' over 350 liters of water a day.
- Trees are able to communicate and defend themselves against attacking insects.

VIDEO: While Watching

Activity 1:

Watch the video and answer these questions.

1. What are the flying rivers?

____

2. What does the flying rivers project do?

____

____

Activity 2:

Watch again. Circle T (true) or F (false) for each sentence. Then correct the false information.

1	**The Amazon Forest pumps carbon dioxide into the atmosphere.**	**T**	**F**
2	**Each tree transpires 3,000 liters of water into the atmosphere every single day.**	**T**	**F**
3	**Rainfall in cities far away is due to the presence of the Amazon Forest.**	**T**	**F**
4	**Some landowners in the rainforest burn down their trees to use the soil for crops or pastures instead.**	**T**	**F**
5	**The Flying Rivers Project has spoken to 650,000 teachers.**	**T**	**F**
6	**We can only destroy 10% more of the Amazon Forest.**	**T**	**F**

VIDEO: After Watching

SPEAKING

1. Read the statement below:

   "The best way to save the Amazon rainforest is through educating young generations."

2. Work in groups. Divide yourselves into two teams.

   Team 1: Write 3 arguments in favor of the statement. Team 2: Write 3 arguments against the statement.

   1. ____
   2. ____
   3. ____

3. Debate your ideas with the other team giving reasons for your points. Use this space to take notes about what the other team says.

   ____

   ____

   ____

   ____

DISCUSSION

Make a group.

Look back at your notes on the debate. Discuss which team(s) you thought delivered the best arguments and why. Then present your results to the class.

WRITING: Critical Thinking

"The Amazon is in danger. Some people have started burning trees to grow food for animals. When this happens, there is less rain in cities around the world."

Step 1: In groups, think of different solutions for this problem.

-
-
-
-

Step 2: Write a report outlining three different solutions to this problem. There are some phrases below to help you.

- In this report I am going to talk about …
- The first solution is …
- The second solution is …
- The problem is …
- … because …
- We should / we shouldn't ...
- In conclusion ...

QUOTABLE QUOTES:

"He that plants trees loves others besides himself."

*By Thomas Fuller**

*Thomas Fuller (1608~1661) English churchman and historian

Look at the quote above. Think about this unit. What do you think the quote means?

VOICE DICTION: Video Shadowing

Watch this section of video (00:20 - 00:40) and underline the stressed words.

"One of the most breathtaking perspectives of the Amazon forest you can ever have is up here, above the canopy ...

... Each one of these trees behind me right now is transpiring between 300 and 1,000 liters of water into the atmosphere every single day."

Now practice saying the sentences out loud.

CRITICAL DISCUSSION

Make groups of 3-4 students. Read each interview one by one. Then ...

- Choose the interviews with the most interesting ideas.
- Prepare to present those to the class in English, explaining why you thought they were the most interesting.

VOCABULARY: Split-Crossword Active Review

Work in pairs.
Each of you has half of today's key words. Ask and give hints in English without saying the word and try to complete the puzzle. See the example below.

A: Excuse me, what is 4 down?
B: Oh, it's a thing you drink from.
A: Do you mean "glass"?
B: Yes, that's right! What is 2 across? ...

Example:

Student A

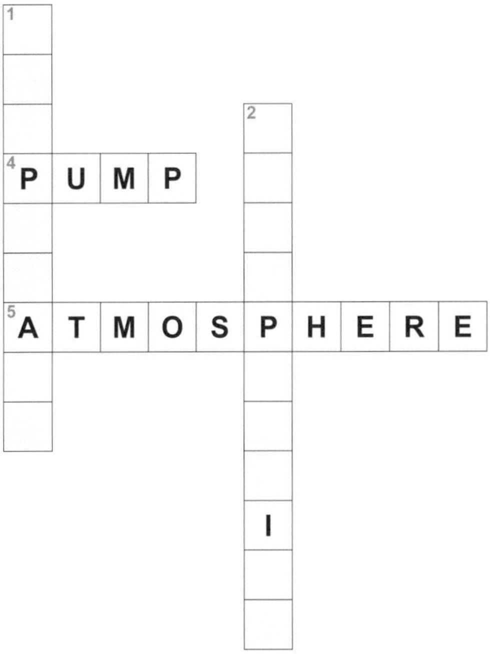

Student B

Now, student A, turn to page **123** and student B, turn to page **130** and try to complete the puzzle using only English.

Optional CLIL Project: Climate change

The Flying Rivers Project and the research it carries out is vital in trying to help fix the problems of climate change.

Make a group. In your group research some of the reasons for climate change.

Then work to produce a PowerPoint or other kind of digital presentation on your research which can be played to the rest of the students in the next class.

CEFR GOALS SELF- EVALUATION	
I can debate about environmental topics.	1---2---3---4---5
I can write a report which gives solutions to a problem.	1---2---3---4---5
I can understand words related to the environment.	1---2---3---4---5
I can understand words related to science.	1---2---3---4---5

Unit 7
Race to the Pole
<Sports>

Learning Goals	Vocabulary from the Video
Speaking Skills: • **presentation** Writing Skills: • **diary entries**	Words related to sports & competition Words related to fitness and health

WARM UP: Talk about it

Work with a partner and try to answer the questions below. Use the internet to check your answers.

1. What amazing human accomplishments do you know about?
2. Why do you think people try so hard to be the best at such dangerous and difficult things?

VOCABULARY: Matching

Match the words and phrases (1-8) and their definitions (a-h).

1. set off	____	a. a distance race when you swim, ride a bike and run
2. epic	____	b. to do something dangerous or foolish
3. extreme athlete	____	c. a person who enjoys adventures and taking risks
4. survival	____	d. unit for measuring the amount of energy in food
5. triathlon	____	e. to start a journey
6. risk	____	f. awe-inspiring, going on for a long time
7. adventurer	____	g. a well-trained person who likes sports which involve risk-taking
8. calories	____	h. act of continuing to exist when facing difficulty

Pushed Output Writing

Now try to write an original sentence using each of the words above.

1. set off ______________________________

____

2. epic ______________________________

____

3. extreme athlete ______________________________

____

4. survival ______________________________

____

5. triathlon ______________________________

____

6. risk ______________________________

____

7. adventurer ______________________________

____

8. calories ______________________________

____

VIDEO: Before Watching

Work in a small group.

1. What do you know about the South Pole?

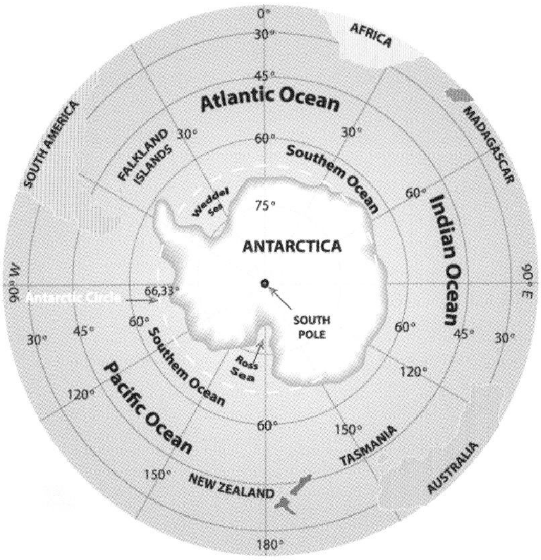

It's in Antarctica.

2. Imagine you are going to travel to the South Pole. What would you take with you? Choose five items.

   1. ______________________
   2. ______________________
   3. ______________________
   4. ______________________
   5. ______________________

VIDEO: While Watching

Activity 1:

Watch the video and discuss the questions.

- What world record is Richard attempting to break?
- Does Richard break the world record?

Activity 2:

Read the questions. Then watch again and answer.

1. What was Richard's previous job?

2. What does Richard love about being an extreme athlete?

3. How long has Richard been training for his journey to the South Pole?

4. What challenges has he faced in preparation for his journey?

5. How many calories will he need from food every day?

6. Where will Richard get the majority of the calories from?

VIDEO: After Watching

SPEAKING

1. Richard loves new challenges. In groups, design a new challenge for him. Use the questions to help you.
   - Where will the challenge take place?
   - What does Richard have to do?
   - What can he take with him?
   - How long does he have to complete the challenge?
2. Now present your challenge to the class.

DISCUSSION

Throughout this unit, you have talked about several different kinds of challenges. As a group, discuss which one was most interesting to you. Now, imagine you had a year's paid vacation to train for and try an unusual challenge. What challenge would you do and how would you prepare for it? Describe your challenge to the class.

WRITING: Critical Thinking

Step 1: Watch the video again from 02:20 to 02:54 without sound. Think about how Richard feels at each stage of the challenge. Make notes.

Step 2: Now use your notes to write a diary entry from Richard's point of view.

QUOTABLE QUOTES:

"It's not the mountain we conquer but ourselves."

*By Sir Edmund Hillary**

* Sir Edmund Hillary (1919~2008) New Zealand mountaineer and explorer and the first man to climb Mt. Everest

Look at the quote above. Think about this unit. What do you think the quote means?

VOICE DICTION: Video Shadowing

1. Watch again from 02:01 to 02:07. What does Richard say? Complete the sentence.
   "And then you've got things like ( ) and ( ) and ( ) and <u>all the other bits</u>."
2. What do you think the underlined words refer to? Give three examples.
3. Now practice saying the sentence out loud until you can do it smoothly.

CRITICAL DISCUSSION

Make groups of 3-4 students. Read each set of diary notes one by one. Then ...

- Choose the diary notes with the most interesting ideas.
- Prepare to present those to the class in English, explaining why you thought they were the most interesting.

VOCABULARY: Split-Crossword Active Review

Work in pairs.
Each of you has half of today's key words. Ask and give hints in English without saying the word and try to complete the puzzle. See the example below.

A: Excuse me, what is 4 down?
B: Oh, it's a thing you drink from.
A: Do you mean "glass"?
B: Yes, that's right! What is 2 across? ...

Example:

Student A

Student B

Now, student A, turn to page **124** and student B, turn to page **131** and try to complete the puzzle using only English.

Optional CLIL Project: World Records

Did you ever look at the Guinness Book of World Records as a child? Do you know anyone who has broken a world record? Have you ever heard of Christian Lopez, who already has more than 30 world records and hopes to eventually have more than 200?

Work in a group. Choose one of the following categories and research different world records in that category:

- Speed records (running, racing, etc)
- Strength
- Food or growing records
- Unusual or funny records

Gather all the information you have collected and then make a poster or presentation with the key facts. Then present the poster to the class.

CEFR GOALS SELF- EVALUATION	
I can give a presentation in front of others.	1---2---3---4---5
I can write diary entries about daily activities.	1---2---3---4---5
I can understand words related to sports & competition.	1---2---3---4---5
I can understand words related to fitness & health.	1---2---3---4---5

Unit 8

Bringing Light

<Science>

Learning Goals	Vocabulary from the Video
Speaking Skills: • **group discussion** Writing Skills: • **making a flyer**	Words related to business Words related to technology

WARM UP: Talk about it

Work with a partner and try to answer the questions below. Use the internet to check your answers.

1. What do you know about solar energy?
2. Do you, your family or your friends use anything with solar power?

VOCABULARY: Matching

Match the words and phrases (1-8) and their definitions (a-h).

1. access	____	a. a liquid fuel for heaters and lamps
2. kerosene	____	b. a way to enter a place
3. fuel	____	c. something that is an integral part of the structure or device
4. LED	____	d. an assembly which uses the sunlight to produce electricity
5. solar panel	____	e. an electronic part that produced light. Light-emitting diode.
6. plug into	____	f. money that is received for work
7. wage	____	g. to connect a device to a power source by inserting a wire
8. built in	____	h. material used to produce heat or power when burned

Pushed Output Writing

Now try to write an original sentence using each of the words above.

1. access ____________________

____

2. kerosene ____________________

____

3. fuel ____________________

____

4. LED ____________________

____

5. solar panel ____________________

____

6. plug into ____________________

____

7. wage ____________________

____

8. built in ____________________

____

VIDEO: Before Watching

Make a list of three things you couldn't live without.

1. ______________________________

2. ______________________________

3. ______________________________

Now compare your list with a partner. Did you choose the same things? What other things can you both not live without?

VIDEO: While Watching

Activity 1:

Watch the video. Are the customers happy with the solar lights? Why or why not?

____

____

Activity 2:

Watch the video again. Complete the gaps with the missing word(s).

1. Kerosene lamps can be ________________ and don't provide much ________________.
2. LEDs are a good solution because they are ________________ and ________________.
3. It is necessary to leave the ________________ in the ________________ to charge.
4. Each light costs ________________ which is more than ________________ the average daily wage.
5. Heidi find out that customers have been ________________ lights to the shop because they are ________________.
6. The redesigned lights will be ________________ to use and ________________ to produce.

VIDEO: After Watching

SPEAKING

1. Write down five things you do when you spend the day at home.
   1. ________________________________
   2. ________________________________
   3. ________________________________
   4. ________________________________
   5. ________________________________
2. Work in groups. Tell each other about your day.
3. Now imagine you had no electricity. How would you plan your day differently? Explain to your group.

DISCUSSION

Over the past decade, there have been many energy-saving improvements to the devices and machines we use in our daily lives. Brainstorm a list of things in your house or life that are marketed as energy-saving or efficient. Taken together, do you think they make a difference in saving our environment? Should we do more? If so, what?

WRITING: Critical Thinking

Step 1: Work in groups. Imagine you work in the marketing department for d.light. Brainstorm four selling points for the new redesigned LED lamps.

-
-
-
-

Step 2: Now design a flyer for the light that could be handed out to people on the streets of Etta. You can use the template below or make your own.

QUOTABLE QUOTES:

"Invention is 1% inspiration and 99% perspiration."

*By Thomas Edison**

* Thomas Edison (1847~1931) American inventor and businessperson

Look at the quote above. Think about this unit. What do you think the quote means?

VOICE DICTION: Video Shadowing

1. Watch the video from 00:42 to 00:47. What does Sam say? Complete the sentence.
   "The LED industry globally has been expanding ( )."
2. Now practice saying the sentence out loud until you can do it smoothly.

CRITICAL DISCUSSION

Make groups of 3-4 students. Read each set of the flyers one by one. Then....

- Choose the flyers with the most interesting ideas.
- Prepare to present those to the class in English, explaining why you thought they were the most interesting.

VOCABULARY: Split-Crossword Active Review

Work in pairs.

Each of you has half of today's key words. Ask and give hints in English without saying the word and try to complete the puzzle. See the example below.

A: Excuse me, what is 4 down?
B: Oh, it's a thing you drink from.
A: Do you mean "glass"?
B: Yes, that's right! What is 2 across? ...

Example:

Student A

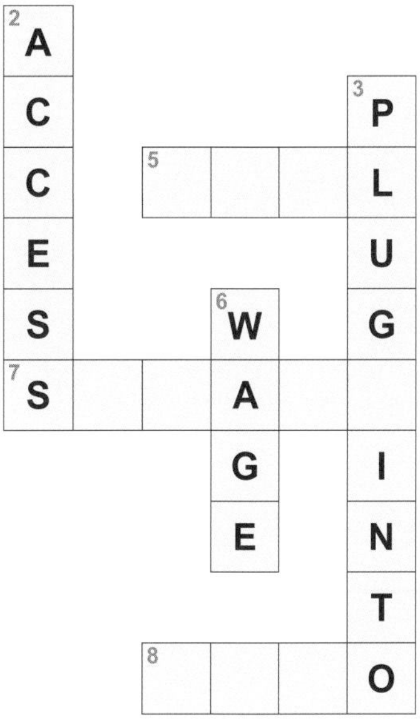

Student B

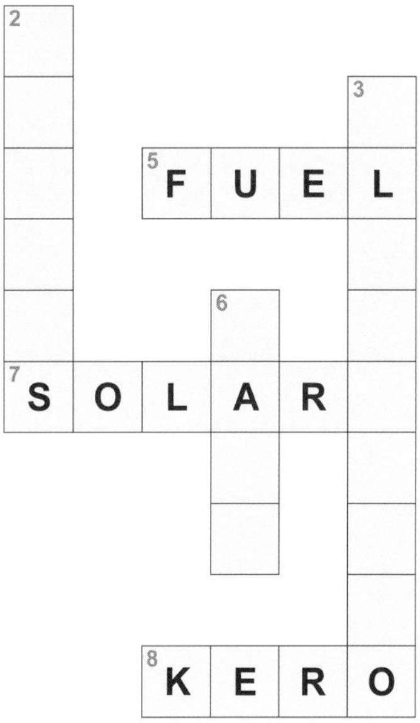

Now, student A, turn to page **124** and student B, turn to page **131** and try to complete the puzzle using only English.

Optional CLIL Project: Progress through technology

Research a company that is using technology in an interesting or unusual way to help improve the developing world (for example, companies that use drones to deliver goods, companies improving access to wifi, the company that makes shoes for children with adjustable sizes, etc.).

Once you have chosen a company and gather all the information you can, work together to make a poster or presentation with the key facts. Be sure to tell the story of the company and explain how the technology improves people's lives in the target country. Then present the poster to the class.

CEFR GOALS SELF- EVALUATION	
I can participate in a group discussion with others.	1---2---3---4---5
I can make a flyer in English.	1---2---3---4---5
I can understand words related to business.	1---2---3---4---5
I can understand words related to technology.	1---2---3---4---5

Unit 9

A Family Business

<Work>

Learning Goals	Vocabulary from the Video
Speaking Skills: • **mingling** Writing Skills: • **making a radio script**	Words related to business Words related to relationships

WARM UP: Talk about it

Work with a partner and try to answer the questions below.

1. What are some of your favorite hair salons? Why do you like them?
2. Did any of them have unusual features to appeal to customers? What were they?

VOCABULARY: Matching

Match the words and phrases (1-8) and their definitions (a-h).

1. community	____	a. to visit someone
2. have a laugh	____	b. a person paying for professional services
3. have in common	____	c. any business that is owned by 2 or more family members
4. socialize	____	d. to have a friendly relationship with someone
5. get along	____	e. to spend time with people; to go out and make friends
6. family-owned	____	f. to share similar interests
7. client	____	g. to joke or behave in a light-hearted manner
8. come by	____	h. a group of people who share a common area or idea

Pushed Output Writing

Now try to write an original sentence using each of the words above.

1. community ____________________

2. have a laugh ____________________

3. have in common ____________________

4. socialize ____________________

5. get along ____________________

6. family-owned ____________________

7. client ____________________

8. come by ____________________

VIDEO: Before Watching

Look at the picture and discuss the questions with a partner.

- What is happening?
- How do you think the people feel?
- What do you think they are talking about?

VIDEO: While Watching

Activity 1:

Why do people go to Tabard Barbers? Watch the video and check all that apply.

a. to escape from the noise and stress of the city
b. to have fun with friends
c. to get their hair cut
d. to learn English
e. to have a coffee

Activity 2:

Watch the video again and answer the questions.

1. What do some people find it hard to do in London?
   a. get a decent haircut
   b. find an apartment in the city center
   c. make friends

2. How long has Tabard Barbers been cutting men's hair?
   a. forty years
   b. seventy-nine years
   c. six years

3. What kind of customers does Tabard Barbers have?
   a. people of all ages
   b. mostly children
   c. young women

4. What was Cece's original plan when she moved to London?
   a. to stay there for six years
   b. to spend six weeks there learning English
   c. to go back home after six months

5. When she first arrived, she ...
   a. couldn't speak English very well.
   b. already knew how to cut hair.
   c. met lots of interesting people.

6. What is the most important thing for Cece?
   a. being the best barber's shop in London
   b. keeping her customers happy
   c. managing a profitable business

7. The narrator says Tabard Barbers is like ...
   a. a big family
   b. the heart of the city
   c. a coffee shop

VIDEO: After Watching

SPEAKING

1. Imagine you have just moved to London. Choose one of the problems and write some notes explaining your situation.
   a. You don't know anybody and you're lonely.
   b. You are finding it difficult to get a job.
   c. Your English isn't very good and you can't understand people.
   d. You don't get on well with your new roommates.
   e. You're feeling stressed because the city is so busy.

   ____

   ____

   ____

2. Work with a partner. Listen to your partner's problem and give them three pieces of advice. Then, explain your problem and listen to the advice your partner gives.
   1. ______________________________
   2. ______________________________
   3. ______________________________

DISCUSSION

Work in a small group.

Tabard Barbers is a successful small business. Do you know of any successful small businesses in your hometown or near your school? Why do you think they were successful? What things should a small business try to do to succeed?

WRITING: Critical Thinking

Step 1: Tabard Barbers has asked you to write the script for an advert* for the local radio station. With a partner, make a list of what you want to include. Think about your target audience and the barber shop's selling points.

*advert abbreviation for an "advertisement" (British) cf. ad. (US)

Step 2: Write a 60-second script with approximately 100 words. Include:

- one or more speakers
- a problem and a solution
- a call to action
- sound effects
- a jingle (optional)

Step 3: Read out your script to the class.

QUOTABLE QUOTES:

"A small business is an amazing way to serve and leave an impact on the world you live in."

*By Nicole Snow**

* Nicole Snow the founder and CEO of Darn Good Yarn

Look at the quote above. Think about this unit. What do you think the quote means?

VOICE DICTION: Video Shadowing

1. Watch the video from 02:21 to 02:28. What does Cece say? Complete the sentence.

   "Tabard Barbers, it's a family business and (   ) ... People, community, (   ) make our customer happy."

2. Now practice saying the sentence out loud until you can do it smoothly.

CRITICAL DISCUSSION

Make groups of 3-4 students. Read each set of the flyers one by one. Then ...

- Choose the flyers with the most interesting ideas.
- Prepare to present those to the class in English, explaining why you thought they were the most interesting.

VOCABULARY: Split-Crossword Active Review

Work in pairs.
Each of you has half of today's key words. Ask and give hints in English without saying the word and try to complete the puzzle. See the example below.

A: Excuse me, what is 4 down?
B: Oh, it's a thing you drink from.
A: Do you mean "glass"?
B: Yes, that's right! What is 2 across? ...

Example:

Student A

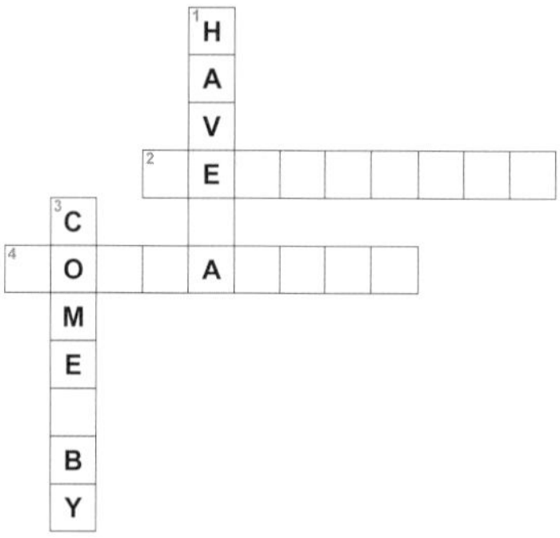

Student B

Now, student A, turn to page **125** and student B, turn to page **132** and try to complete the puzzle using only English.

Optional CLIL Project: A business plan

Work in a group to plan a small business. Brainstorm and discuss any gaps there might be in the market in your local area. Try to be original and imaginative but also practical. Choose and idea you think might be successful.

Next, discuss the details of the business and then make a business plan. This should include:

- a name
- company description
- market analysis (who are your target customers?)
- products and services
- finances (how much money will you need to start with?)

Finally, create a presentation and share your business plan with the class

CEFR GOALS SELF- EVALUATION	
I can give advice to others in English.	1---2---3---4---5
I can make a radio script in English.	1---2---3---4---5
I can understand words related to business.	1---2---3---4---5
I can understand words related to relationships.	1---2---3---4---5

Unit 10
Heston We Have a Problem
<Food>

Learning Goals	Vocabulary from the Video
Speaking Skills: ● **discussion** Writing Skills: ● **making a menu card**	Words related to space Words related to food

WARM UP: Talk about it

Work with a partner and try to answer the questions below.

1. Have you ever gone on a long hike or trip far away from stores and restaurants? What did you take to eat?
2. When you have no time for a proper meal, what do you eat?

VOCABULARY: Matching

Match the words and phrases (1-8) and their definitions (a-h).

1. orbiting	____	a. a special assignment given to a person or group
2. astronaut	____	b. when a person becomes weightless, usually in space
3. mission	____	c. to go around another object (often in space)
4. zero gravity	____	d. a person who travels in space
5. solar system	____	e. a shortened form of refrigerator, the cold place you keep food
6. pouch	____	f. the part of a refrigerator that operates below zero degrees
7. fridge	____	g. the collection of 8 planets and moons orbiting our sun
8. freezer	____	h. a small, flexible bag

Pushed Output Writing

Now try to write an original sentence using each of the words above.

1. orbiting ____

____

2. astronaut ____

____

3. mission ____

____

4. zero gravity ____

____

5. solar system ____

____

6. pouch ____

____

7. fridge ____

____

8. freezer ____

____

VIDEO: Before Watching

In pairs, discuss what challenges people might have in space. Then fill in the mind map below:

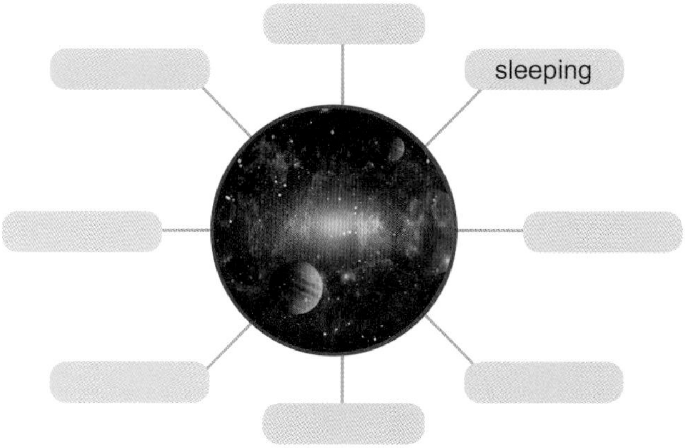

VIDEO: While Watching

Activity 1:

Watch the video. Who are the men in the photos? How are they connected?

Activity 2:

Watch the video again. Read the advert for Tim's favorite food, and complete the information.

TIRED OF BORING OLD SPACE FOOD?
TRY OUR DELICIOUS NEW RECIPE!*

*Created by 1. __________ chef Heston Blumenthal.

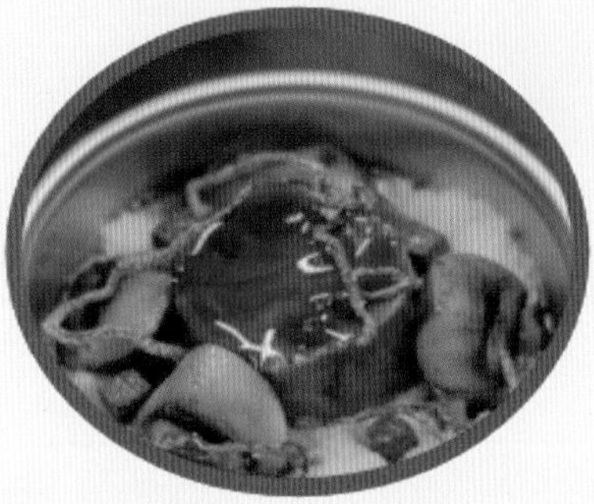

SAUSAGE AND
2. ______________
POTATOES.

- Excellent for surviving the long journey to space - no need for a fridge or 3. __________
- It comes perfectly packaged in a small pouch or 4. __________.
- It's the parfect 5. __________ of home!
- Lasts for 6. __________.
- Can survive in zero 7. __________ conditions.

Recommended by the British 8. __________

Tim Peake - "It tastes absolutely 9. __________, really wonderful!"

VIDEO: After Watching

SPEAKING

Space food must be nutritious, easily digestible, light, well packaged, fast to serve, store well, easy to open, have minimal cleanup, easy to cook, have good taste, and leave minimal waste.

1. Discuss in groups which of the items on the menu card would be appropriate for space, and why?

2. Work in pairs. Create your own menu card for the International Space Station. Include some of your favorite meals from home.

MENU

- ☑ **Freeze-dried strawberries**
- ☑ **Bacon bars**
- ☑ **Fresh bread**
- ☑ **Tortillab bread**
- ☑ **Sandwich cubes**
- ☑ **Spaghetti with meat sauce**
- ☑ **Hot Sauce**
- ☑ **Carton of strawberry yoghurt**
- ☑ **Sugar coated chocolates**
- ☑ **Powdered juices**
- ☑ **Still lemonade**
- ☑ **Orange soda**
- ☑ **Instant tea / coffee**

MENU

- ☐
- ☐
- ☐
- ☐
- ☐
- ☐
- ☐
- ☐
- ☐
- ☐
- ☐
- ☐

DISCUSSION

Work in a small group.

Do you know how to cook? What is the most delicious thing you know how to make? Tell your group the recipe and describe how to make it.

WRITING: Critical Thinking

Choose one of the dishes from the menu card on the previous page and write a recipe card. Think about how it would need to be modified for space. Use some of the useful language below.

Verbs:	*add*	*pour*	*mix*	*seal*	*serve*	*free-dry*	*dehydrate*
Containers:	*tin*	*pouch*	*carton*	*bag*			
Stages:	*First,*	*Next,*	*Then,*	*After,*	*Finally*		

Recipe

1

2

3

4

5

QUOTABLE QUOTES:

"When I orbited the Earth in a spaceship, I saw for the first time how beautiful our planet is. Mankind, let us preserve and increase this beauty, and not destroy it!"

*By Yuri Gagarin**

* Yuri Gagarin (1934~1968) former Soviet pilot and cosmonaut who became the first human to journey into outer space

Look at the quote above. Think about this unit. What do you think the quote means?

VOICE DICTION: Video Shadowing

1. Watch the video from 01:04 to 01:07. What does Heston say? Complete the sentence.

   “You can make that food taste ( ) better, an ( ) better.”

2. Now practice saying the sentence out loud until you can do it smoothly.

CRITICAL DISCUSSION

Make groups of 3-4 students. Read each recipe card one by one. Then …

- Choose the most delicious sounding recipe card.
- Prepare to present to the class in English, explaining why you thought it was the most interesting.

VOCABULARY: Split-Crossword Active Review

Work in pairs.
Each of you has half of today’s key words. Ask and give hints in English without saying the word and try to complete the puzzle. See the example below.

A: Excuse me, what is 4 down?
B: Oh, it's a thing you drink from.
A: Do you mean “glass”?
B: Yes, that's right! What is 2 across? ...

Example:

Student A

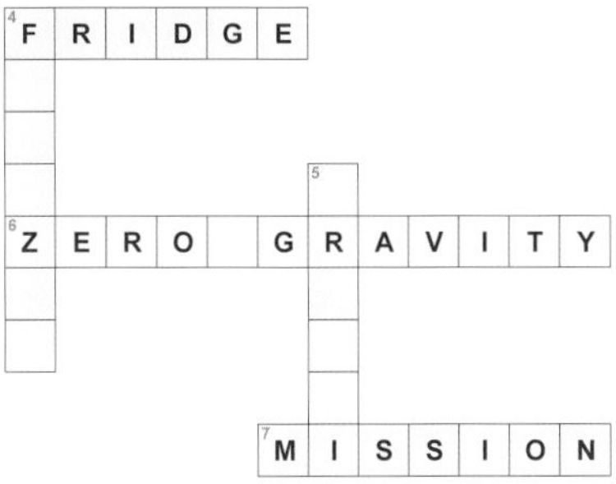

Student B

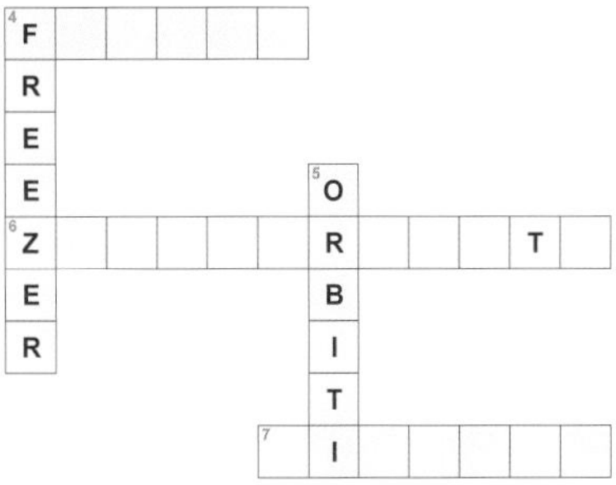

Now, student A, turn to page **125** and student B, turn to page **132** and try to complete the puzzle using only English.

Optional CLIL Project: Space food experiment

Work in small groups. In this experiment you are going to make a space pudding, just like what the astronauts eat in space. You will need the following ingredients and equipment:

- Instant cake / pudding mix or chocolate drinking powder
- Powdered milk
- Water
- Ziploc plastic bags
- Measuring spoons
- Measuring cup

* Ziploc "a brand name for a type of plastic bag that can be closed firmly by pressing the two edges at the top together, and opened by pulling them apart" (Cambridge Dictionary)

Next, read the directions below and make the pudding.

1. Put one tablespoon plus two teaspoons of dry pudding mix into the zip lock bag.
2. Add the same amount of powdered milk into the bag.
3. Mix (this is how it would arrive at the space station).
4. Pour in 1/2 cup of water and seal the bag.
5. Squeeze the mixture until it's all mixed together.
6. Cut the corner of the bag.
7. Enjoy your space pudding!

Finally, write up the experiment including your findings.

CEFR GOALS SELF- EVALUATION	
I can talk about food in English.	1---2---3---4---5
I can make a menu card in English.	1---2---3---4---5
I can understand words related to space.	1---2---3---4---5
I can understand words related to food.	1---2---3---4---5

Unit 11
Cops on the Job
<Work>

Learning Goals	Vocabulary from the Video
Speaking Skills: • **roleplay** Writing Skills: • **police report**	Words related to crime & punishment Words related to work

WARM UP: Talk about it

Work with a partner and try to answer the questions below.

1. What is your favorite police movie or drama?
2. Why do you like them?

VOCABULARY: Matching

Match the words and phrases (1-8) and their definitions (a-h).

1. cop	____	a.	to enter somewhere illegally
2. incident	____	b.	buildings and the areas or lands it rests on
3. premises	____	c.	an unusual or important event or accident
4. break into	____	d.	another word for police officer
5. burglar	____	e.	someone who is good at doing many different things
6. red-handed	____	f.	a person you work with
7. colleague	____	g.	to be caught in the act of doing something wrong
8. Jack-of-all-trades	____	h.	a thief who enters a building with the hope to steal something

Pushed Output Writing

Now try to write an original sentence using each of the words above.

1. cop ____________________

2. incident ____________________

3. premises ____________________

4. break into ____________________

5. burglar ____________________

6. red-handed ____________________

7. colleague ____________________

8. Jack-of-all-trades ____________________

VIDEO: Before Watching

What are some of the things you think police officers do on a typical day at work? Discuss in groups and then complete the diagram.

VIDEO: While Watching

Activity 1:

Watch the video about PC Carla Rossi and PC Marc Louis. Were any of your ideas from the previous activity mentioned? Write them down.

____

____

What other things are mentioned? Write them down.

____

____

Activity 2:

Watch the video again. Complete the gaps with words from the video.

1. A cop never knows what kind of emergency they'll ______________________ next.
2. If a horse had run away, it could ______________________ an accident.
3. As people call the police in all kinds of situations, PC Carla Rossi ______________________.
4. When there is a burglar inside a premises, you really wanna ______________________ red-handed.
5. While the police have been trapped, the burglar's ______________________ lots of stock.
6. Not everything ______________________ for the police.

VIDEO: After Watching

SPEAKING

Work in pairs. Imagine you are PC Marc Louis and his colleague who got trapped in the shop. Your boss has asked you to explain what happened. First think of some questions he might ask you.

1. ______________________________

____

2. ______________________________

____

3. ______________________________

____

4. ______________________________

____

Now roleplay the conversation with your partner. Decide who will be PC Marc and who will be his boss. Then, switch roles.

DISCUSSION

Work in a small group.

How are police viewed in your country? Do they try to interact with and get to know people in the community? Have you ever met or spoken with someone working for the police? What was your impression?

WRITING: Critical Thinking

Imagine you are PC Carla Rossi. You have been asked to write up the report on the 'horse incident'.

1. Work in pairs. Make notes on the incident.

2. Now write your police report. Remember, a police report must:

- be factual
- be a descriptive account of what happened
- use formal language
- include the passive voice where possible

POLICE REPORT

Case No:

Date:

Reporting Officer:

Prepared by:

INCIDENT:

DETAILS OF EVENT:

ACTION TAKEN:

SUMMARY:

QUOTABLE QUOTES:

"People sleep peacefully in their beds at night only because rough men stand ready to do violence on their behalf."

*By George Orwell**

* George Orwell (1903~1950) English novelist and essayist

Look at the quote above. Think about this unit. What do you think the quote means?

VOICE DICTION: Video Shadowing

1. Watch the video from 01:21 to 01:26. What does PC Carla Rossi say? Complete the sentence.

   "You know, and I just think it's (   ), 'cause, we're kind of (   ) really."

2. Now practice saying the sentence out loud until you can do it smoothly.

CRITICAL DISCUSSION

Make groups of 3-4 students. Read each police report one by one. Then ...

- Choose the reports with the most interesting ideas.
- Prepare to present those to the class in English, explaining why you thought they were the most interesting.

VOCABULARY: Split-Crossword Active Review

Work in pairs.
Each of you has half of today's key words. Ask and give hints in English without saying the word and try to complete the puzzle. See the example below.

A: Excuse me, what is 4 down?
B: Oh, it's a thing you drink from.
A: Do you mean "glass"?
B: Yes, that's right! What is 2 across? ...

Example:

Student A

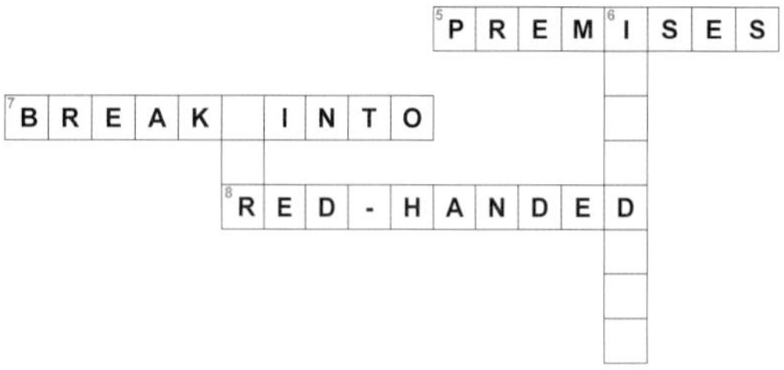

Student B

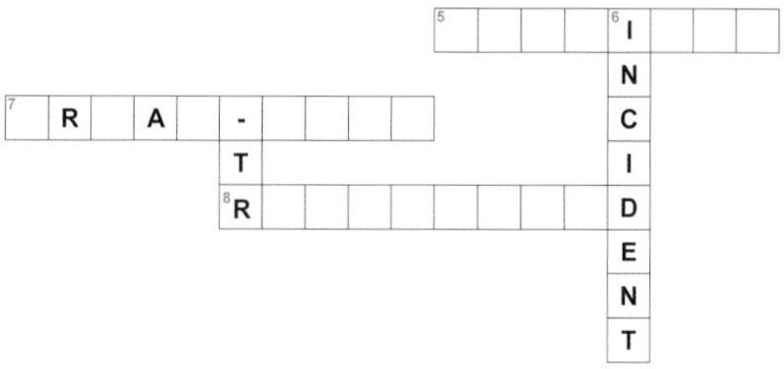

Now, student A, turn to page **126** and student B, turn to page **133** and try to complete the puzzle using only English.

Optional CLIL Project: Uniforms

All police forces around the world have a uniform, but why?

Work in small groups and research the reasons why the police wear uniforms. You should also find out about how police uniforms have changed over the years and how they vary from country to country. Include a labelled diagram of some of the different components of police uniforms, and their functions.

Once you have conducted your research, your group should produce a glossy magazine-style article with informative text and lots of pictures.

Finally, you should present your articles to the rest of the class and vote on which police uniforms are the best, most suitable, most fashionable etc.

CEFR GOALS SELF- EVALUATION	
I can do a role play in English.	1---2---3---4---5
I can write a police report in English.	1---2---3---4---5
I can understand words related to crime and punishment.	1---2---3---4---5
I can understand words related to work.	1---2---3---4---5

Unit 12

Things I've Learned About Failure <Life>

Learning Goals	Vocabulary from the Video
Speaking Skills: • **presentation** Writing Skills: • **letter writing**	Words related to success Words related to failure

WARM UP: Talk about it

Work with a partner and try to answer the questions below.

1. Did you ever have a dream to be a musician, an actor or some other difficult-to-achieve job?
2. Did you try to get this job? Why or why not? How did it go?

VOCABULARY: Matching

Match the words and phrases (1-8) and their definitions (a-h).

1. fulfill a dream	____	a. to achieve something you wanted for a long time
2. achieve a goal	____	b. to be able to do what you dreamed of doing
3. realize an ambition	____	c. to succeed in making a specific aim happen
4. mess up	____	d. when something happens differently than you expected
5. overcome a problem	____	e. a situation where you feel safe or at ease
6. missed opportunity	____	f. to not use a chance to do something
7. comfort zone	____	g. to work through a challenge to achieve a goal
8. not go according to plan	____	h. to make a mistake

Pushed Output Writing

Now try to write an original sentence using each of the words above.

1. fulfill a dream ______________________________

____

2. achieve a goal ______________________________

____

3. realize an ambition ______________________________

____

4. mess up ______________________________

____

5. overcome a problem ______________________________

____

6. missed opportunity ______________________________

____

7. comfort zone ______________________________

____

8. not go according to plan ______________________________

____

VIDEO: Before Watching

"If at first you don't succeed, try, try again."

Look at the phrase above and discuss the questions with a partner.

1. What do you think the phrase means?
2. Do you have a similar saying in your language?
3. Is this usually your approach to trying new things? Why (not)?

VIDEO: While Watching

Activity 1:

Watch the video and order the advice Ben gives. Write the number in the box.

A. Allow yourself time to achieve your goals - it may take longer than you expect.
B. Enjoy the incredible sense of satisfaction you'll get when you do fulfil a dream.
C. Learning what you don't want to do is as important as recognizing your dreams.
D. Reflect on missed opportunities so you know what to do next time.
E. Stepping out of your comfort zone is important when realizing a dream.

1. ☐ → 2. ☐ → 3. ☐ → 4. ☐ → 5. ☐

Activity 2:

Watch the video again. Circle T (true) or F (false) for each sentence. Then correct the false information.

1	**Ben believes you learn from making mistakes.**	**T**	**F**
2	**When he was younger, he always had lots of dreams he wanted to fulfil.**	**T**	**F**
3	**He tried to release an album of electronic music, but it didn't go to plan.**	**T**	**F**
4	**He thinks it's a bad idea to ask 'What if?' after something's happened.**	**T**	**F**
5	**His experience of doing stand-up comedy made him realize it wasn't a dream he wanted to fulfil.**	**T**	**F**
6	**He says achieving your goal will probably be easier and take less time than you imagine.**	**T**	**F**

VIDEO: After Watching

SPEAKING

You are going to tell your partner about a goal you've achieved. Look at the questions and think about what you're going to say.

- What was the dream you wanted to fulfil?
- How long did it take you to achieve your goal?
- What difficulties did you have along the way? How did you overcome them?
- How did you feel when you achieved your goal?

Now, listen to your partner. As they're speaking, ask at least three follow-up questions to find out more information.

DISCUSSION

Discuss the following in a small group.

How hard do you think it is to become a professional musician, actor or athlete? What kind of things do you think they need to do in order to succeed?

WRITING: Critical Thinking

A friend of yours is studying English and wants to be good enough to be able to go abroad to an English-speaking country to go to school. Based on your own experience and ideas about learning English, write a letter to him and give him some advice to help him achieve his goal.

QUOTABLE QUOTES:

"There will be obstacles. There will be doubters. There will be mistakes. But with hard work, there are no limits."

By Michael Phelps

Do you know who Michael Phelps is? Do a quick check on the internet and then look at the quote above. Think about this unit. What do you think the quote means?

VOICE DICTION: Video Shadowing

1. Watch the video from 01:46 to 01:51. What does Ben say? Complete the sentence.

   "Do you ever ( ) to a memory and realize: 'Oh!
   I ( ) there?'"

2. Now practice saying the sentence out loud until you can do it smoothly.

CRITICAL DISCUSSION

Make groups of 3-4 students. Read each letter one by one. Then ...

- Choose the letters with the most interesting ideas.
- Prepare to present those to the class in English, explaining why you thought they were the most interesting.

VOCABULARY: Split-Crossword Active Review

Work in pairs.

Each of you has half of today's key words. Ask and give hints in English without saying the word and try to complete the puzzle. See the example below.

A: Excuse me, what is 4 down?
B: Oh, it's a thing you drink from.
A: Do you mean "glass"?
B: Yes, that's right! What is 2 across? ...

Example:

Student A

Student B

Now, student A, turn to page **126** and student B, turn to page **133** and try to complete the puzzle using only English.

Optional CLIL Project: Study Guide

In the video, Ben gave advice for achieving your goals. In this project, you will work in a group to create a study guide for a specific subject to give learners advice on how to do well in that area.

As a class, use the whiteboard and discuss what learners find easy and challenging when studying. For the areas you find challenging, try also to brainstorm ideas on ways to overcome those problems.

Now work in small groups with each group choosing a different school subject.
Work together to design a leaflet for fellow learners with appropriate study skills for that subject.
When designing your leaflet, consider:

- how you can study the subject regularly
- how to organize notes
- how to record keywords and terms
- how to draw a timetable for exam revision and deadlines

Remember, study guides should be informative and easy-to-read.
Please feel free to use images to support the tips they provide.

CEFR GOALS SELF- EVALUATION	
I can give a presentation in English.	1---2---3---4---5
I can write a letter in English.	1---2---3---4---5
I can understand words related to success.	1---2---3---4---5
I can understand words related to failure.	1---2---3---4---5

Unit 13
Powwow: A Gathering for Native Americans <Culture>

Learning Goals	Vocabulary from the Video
Speaking Skills: ● **presentation** Writing Skills: ● **article**	Words related to celebrations Words related to music

WARM UP: Talk about it

Work with a partner and answer the questions below.

1. Are there any people or groups that are native to Japan?
2. What do you know about their culture, customs, food and history?

VOCABULARY: Matching

Match the words and phrases (1-8) and their definitions (a-h).

1. celebration	____	a. the act of people meeting again after being apart for awhile
2. gathering	____	b. to decide to take part in some activity
3. reunion	____	c. a party or event where people are rejoicing about something
4. join in	____	d. a meeting of people who come together
5. flowing	____	e. staying in harmony with the pulse of the music
6. pitch	____	f. having a pleasant sound
7. melodic	____	g. a sound at a particular level
8. on beat	____	h. to move steadily or easily in a certain direction

Pushed Output Writing

Now try to write an original sentence using each of the words above.

1. celebration ______________________________

____

2. gathering ______________________________

____

3. reunion ______________________________

____

4. join in ______________________________

____

5. flowing ______________________________

____

6. pitch ______________________________

____

7. melodic ______________________________

____

8. on beat ______________________________

____

VIDEO: Before Watching

Look at the pictures. Who do you think is a Native American? Discuss with a partner, giving reasons for your answers.

1.

2.

3.

VIDEO: While Watching

Activity 1:

What do people do at the Powwow? Make notes.

Activity 2:

Watch again. Read the sentences and correct any mistakes.

1. A single tribe meets and celebrates together at a Powwow.
2. Early contact with the Europeans caused the tribe to lose their identity.
3. There are two types of drumming: Northern Style, which is lower pitch and melodic, and Southern Style, which is higher pitch and has a clear attitude.
4. The drum helps Sunshine disconnect from the problems she faces in her life.
5. Mickela is given the following advice when learning to dance: stay on the beat, know the song, keep her arms out like a butterfly.
6. The Powwow allows the community to celebrate and share their culture with each other.

VIDEO: After Watching

SPEAKING

Think about a celebration or festival you have attended. Describe your experience to your group. Say:

- When and where it took place
- How people celebrated, e.g. dance,
- music, food, clothing
- What you enjoyed about it

DISCUSSION

Discuss the following in a small group.

Based on what you have studied and heard (you can also check the internet while you are discussing), do you think Native Americans were treated fairly throughout American history? How about the native peoples of your land? Why do you think these injustices happen?

WRITING: Critical Thinking

Try to remember as much as you can about the Powwow. If necessary, watch the video again and make notes.

Imagine you went to the Powwow. Use your notes to write an article about it. Try to include:

- a question or interesting fact to get the reader's attention
- detailed description of the atmosphere
- the reasons why the Powwow is celebrated
- quotes from people at the event
- your opinions and conclusions about the Powwow

Dossier

Magazine

1

QUOTABLE QUOTES:

"When we show our respect for other living things, they respond with respect for us."

— native American saying

Think about this unit. What do you think the quote means?

VOICE DICTION: Video Shadowing

1. Watch the video from 00:40 to 00:47. What does the Lumbee tribe member say? Complete the sentence.

   "That's one thing our ancestors ( ): 'You are Native American. You keep that ( ) happens.'"

2. Now practice saying the sentence out loud until you can do it smoothly.

CRITICAL DISCUSSION

Make groups of 3-4 students. Read each letter one by one. Then ...

- Choose the letters with the most interesting ideas.
- Prepare to present those to the class in English, explaining why you thought they were the most interesting.

VOCABULARY: Split-Crossword Active Review

Work in pairs.
Each of you has half of today's key words. Ask and give hints in English without saying the word and try to complete the puzzle. See the example below.

A: Excuse me, what is 4 down?
B: Oh, it's a thing you drink from.
A: Do you mean “glass”?
B: Yes, that's right! What is 2 across? ...

Example:

Student A

Student B

Now, student A, turn to page **127** and student B, turn to page **134** and try to complete the puzzle using only English.

Optional CLIL Project: Native American Languages

Many Native American languages have been lost or are in danger of disappearing. For this project you will plan and teach a lesson in a Native American language.

Work in a small group. Then choose one of the following languages and find some simple phrases and vocabulary to teach your classmates. You can use online videos and apps to help you find the words and learn the correct pronunciation.

- Navajo
- Quechua
- Cherokee
- Inuktitut (Inuit)

Choose the words and phrases you want to teach and then think about the order you want to teach them and how you would like to teach them. You can prepare a poster or PowerPoint presentation to make it easier for the students to learn.

CEFR GOALS SELF- EVALUATION	
I can give a presentation in English.	1---2---3---4---5
I can write an article in English.	1---2---3---4---5
I can understand words related to celebrations.	1---2---3---4---5
I can understand words related to music.	1---2---3---4---5

Unit 14

Wildlife Filmmaker

<Work>

Learning Goals	Vocabulary from the Video
Speaking Skills: • **discussion** Writing Skills: • **article**	Words related to film & photography Words related to wildlife

WARM UP: Talk about it

Work with a partner and answer the questions below.

1. What African wildlife do you know of?
2. Which animals are you most interested in? Why?

VOCABULARY: Matching

Match the words and phrases (1-8) and their definitions (a-h).

1. habitat	____	a. very physically near to a person or animal
2. game reserve	____	b. to fix a device into a specific place
3. hyena	____	c. a film that gives facts about a person, place or event
4. scavenger	____	d. a small, high definition, waterproof camera
5. documentary	____	e. a wild animal from Africa that looks like a dog
6. GoPro	____	f. an animal that feeds on dead animal meat
7. to rig up	____	g. a large area of land where wild animals live safely
8. up close and personal	____	h. a natural place where plants or animals live

Pushed Output Writing

Now try to write an original sentence using each of the words above.

1. habitat ______________________________

____

2. game reserve ______________________________

____

3. hyena ______________________________

____

4. scavenger ______________________________

____

5. documentary ______________________________

____

6. GoPro ______________________________

____

7. to rig up ______________________________

____

8. up close and personal ______________________________

____

VIDEO: Before Watching

1. Work in pairs. Look at the idiom below. What do you think it means?

2. Do you have a similar expression in your language? What other animal idioms do you know?

VIDEO: While Watching

Activity 1:

Watch the video. Discuss the question in pairs. Is a hyena:

a. a wolf in sheep's clothing?
b. a sheep in wolf's clothing?

Activity 2:

Watch the video again. Answer the questions.

1. Where does Kim Wolhuter show the animals in the documentaries that he makes?
2. How many different GoPro cameras does he mention?
3. Where is the Mushatu game reserve situated?
4. Where do the hyenas hang out in the game reserve?
5. Kim Wolhuter says that hyenas are "labelled dirty, dangerous and scavengers". Why does he think hyenas have these labels?
6. How long has he been filming these hyenas?

VIDEO: After Watching

SPEAKING

Discuss the questions in pairs.

1. Have you seen any interesting wildlife documentaries recently?
2. Why do you think these documentaries are made? Is there any purpose beyond making money?
3. Do you think you are maverick and eccentric enough to be a wildlife filmmaker? Are these qualities necessary or useful for the job?

DISCUSSION

Discuss the following in a small group.

- Are there any wild animals that you would like to get up close and personal with?
- Do you prefer animals that are gentle and caring or scavengers?
- In your opinion, what other animals are misunderstood?

WRITING: Critical Thinking

Work in groups. In the video we learn that hyenas have a reputation that is not deserved. Brainstorm other things that have this problem.

Now write a magazine article entitled "Common Myths Debunked" explaining and correcting these misunderstandings. Make sure you:

- write a question or interesting fact to hook the reader's attention
- use a friendly and chatty tone
- try to include one or two rhetorical questions

QUOTABLE QUOTES:

"The love for all creatures is the most noble attribute of man."

by Charles Darwin

* Charles Darwin (1809~1882) English naturalist who advocated the theory of evolution

Think about this unit. What do you think the quote means?

VOICE DICTION: Video Shadowing

1. Watch the video from 01:12 to 01:17. What does the Lumbee tribe member say? Complete the sentence.

   "For my work I get ( ) animals and Mashatu is the ( )."

2. Now practice saying the sentence out loud until you can do it smoothly.

CRITICAL DISCUSSION

Make groups of 3-4 students. Read each letter one by one. Then ...

- Choose the letters with the most interesting ideas.
- Prepare to present those to the class in English, explaining why you thought they were the most interesting.

VOCABULARY: Split-Crossword Active Review

Work in pairs.

Each of you has half of today's key words. Ask and give hints in English without saying the word and try to complete the puzzle. See the example below.

A: Excuse me, what is 4 down?

B: Oh, it's a thing you drink from.

A: Do you mean "glass"?

B: Yes, that's right! What is 2 across? ...

Example:

Student A

Student B

Now, student A, turn to page **127** and student B, turn to page **134** and try to complete the puzzle using only English.

Optional CLIL Project: Misunderstood Animals

Many animals around the world are mistreated and killed because the people they share the environment with don't understand them.

Make a group. Research this issue and then decide on an animal you want to research in more depth. Some animals that are misunderstood include bees, sharks, mountain lions, wolves and killer whales.

One you have chosen an animal, find out about their habits, routines and characteristics and make a leaflet that could be used to inform people that live close to it.

CEFR GOALS SELF- EVALUATION	
I can have a discussion about wildlife in English.	1---2---3---4---5
I can write an article in English.	1---2---3---4---5
I can understand words related to film & photography.	1---2---3---4---5
I can understand words related to wildlife.	1---2---3---4---5

Split-Crossword (student A)

Unit 1

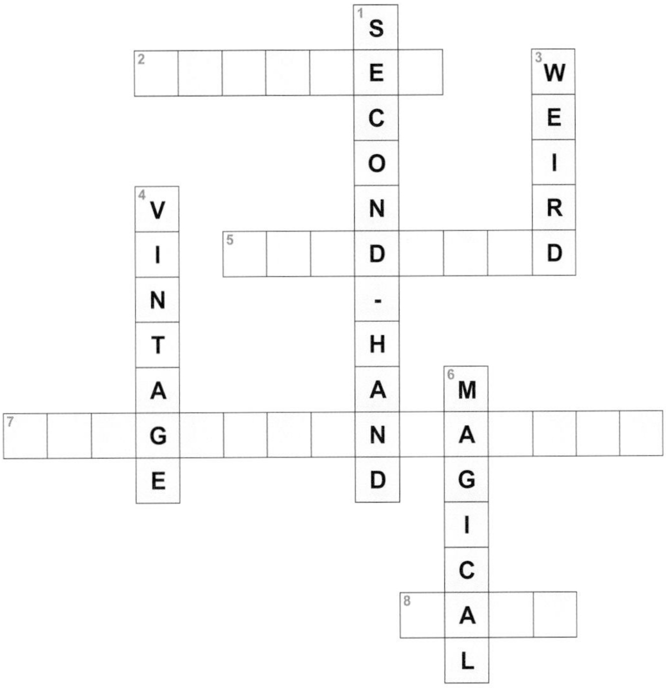

Unit 2

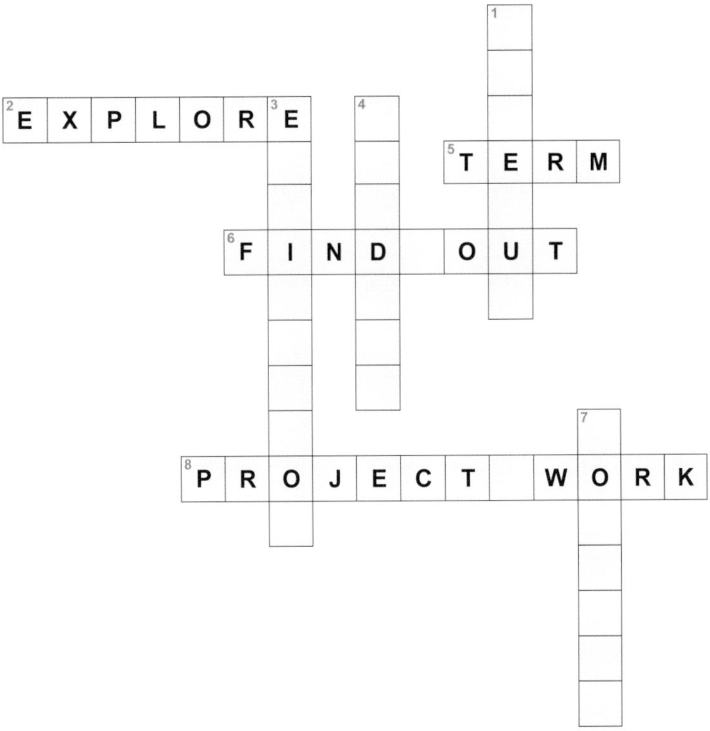

Unit 3

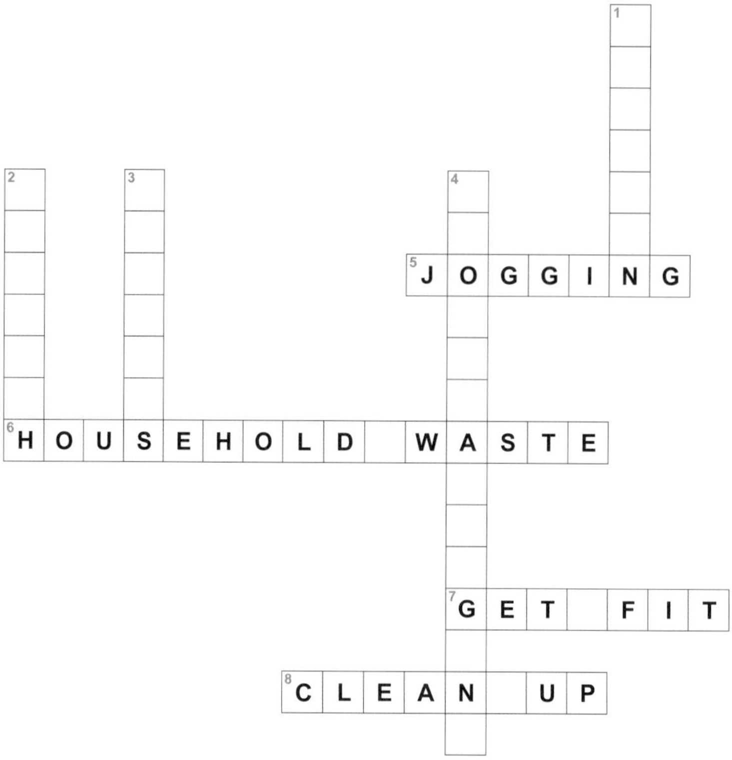
1
2
3
4
5 JOGGING
6 HOUSEHOLD WASTE
7 GET FIT
8 CLEAN UP

Unit 4

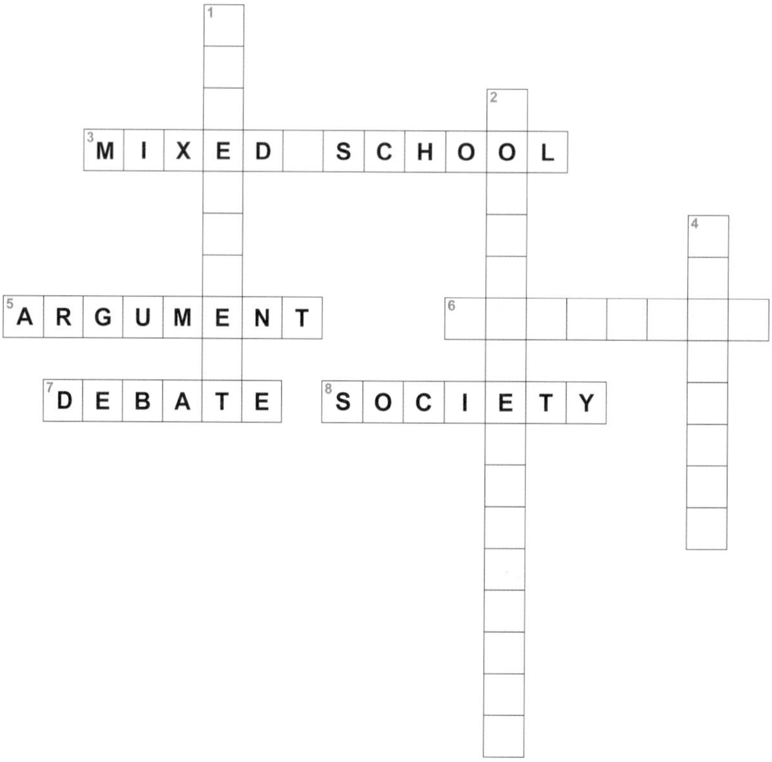
1
2
3 MIXED SCHOOL
4
5 ARGUMENT
6
7 DEBATE
8 SOCIETY

Unit 5

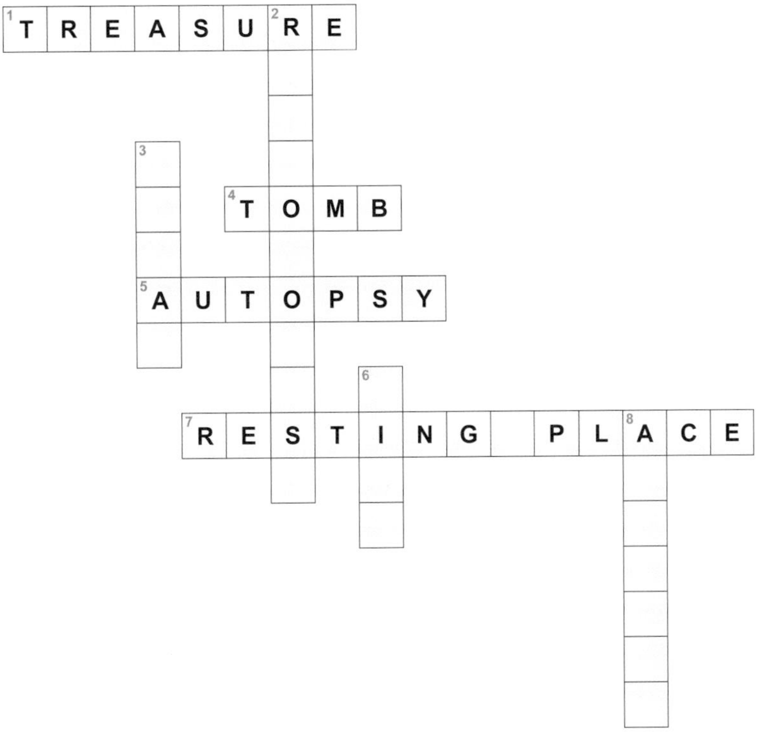
1 TREASURE
2
3
4 TOMB
5 AUTOPSY
6
7 RESTING PLACE
8

Unit 6

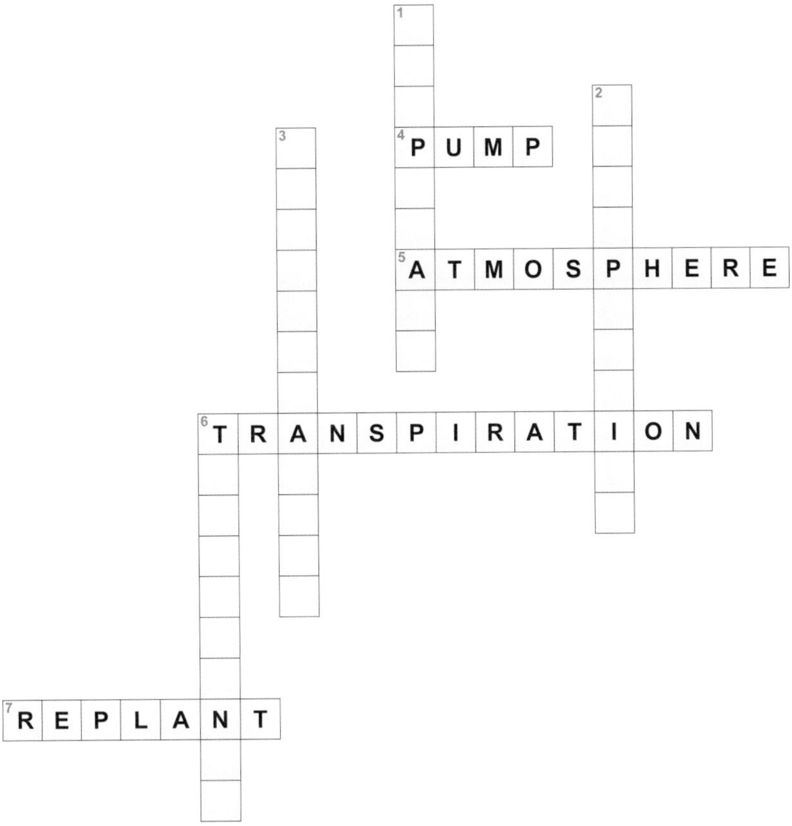
1
2
3
4 PUMP
5 ATMOSPHERE
6 TRANSPIRATION
7 REPLANT

Unit 7

TRIATHLON
CALORIES
SURVIVAL
ADVENTURER

Unit 8

BUILT
IN
ACCESS
PLUG
INTO
WAGE

Unit 9

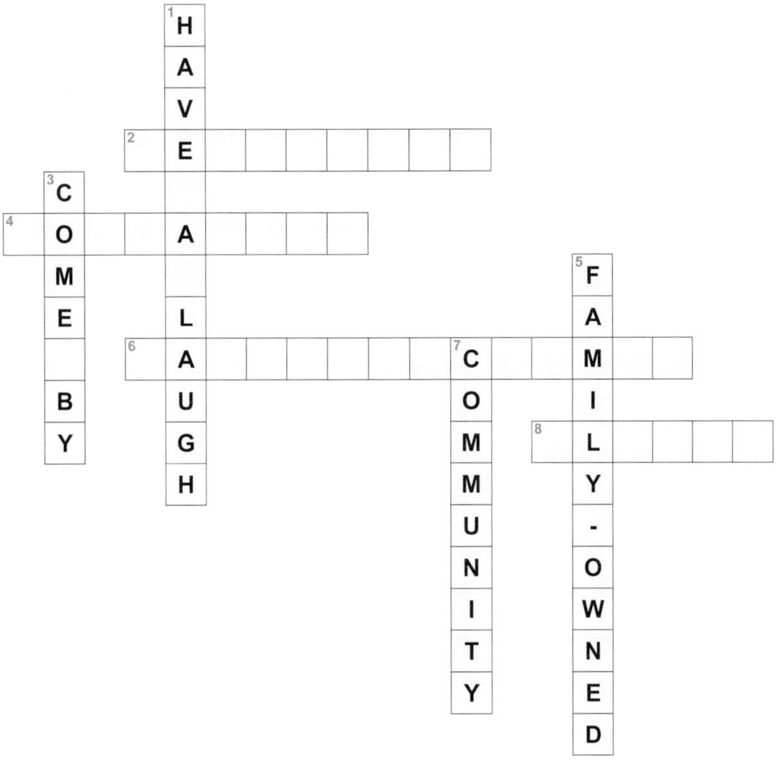

Unit 10

Unit 11

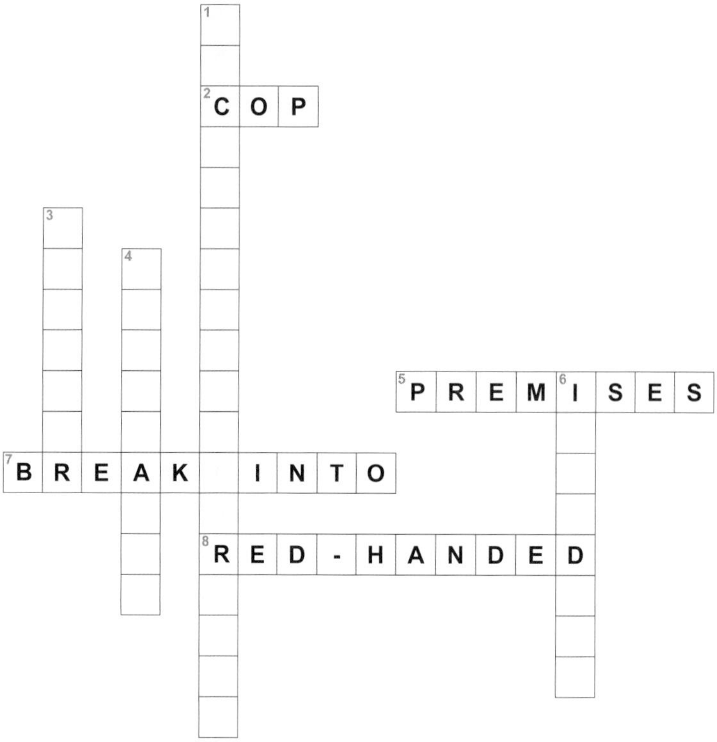

Unit 12

Unit 13

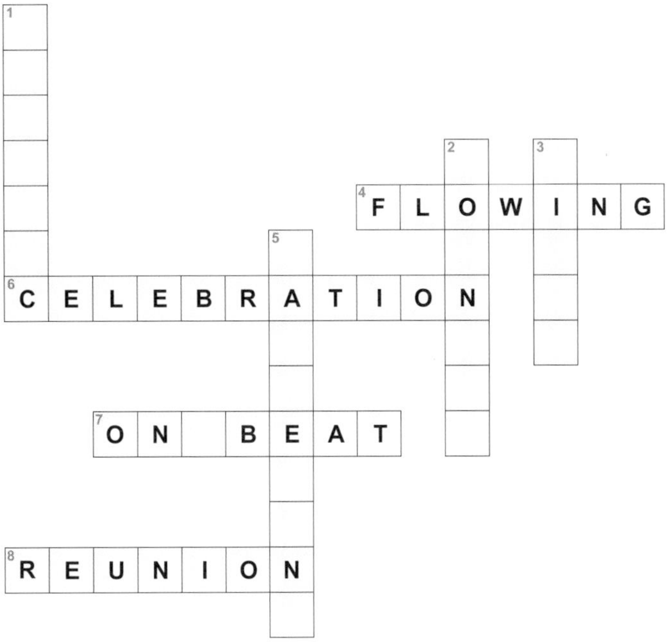

Unit 14

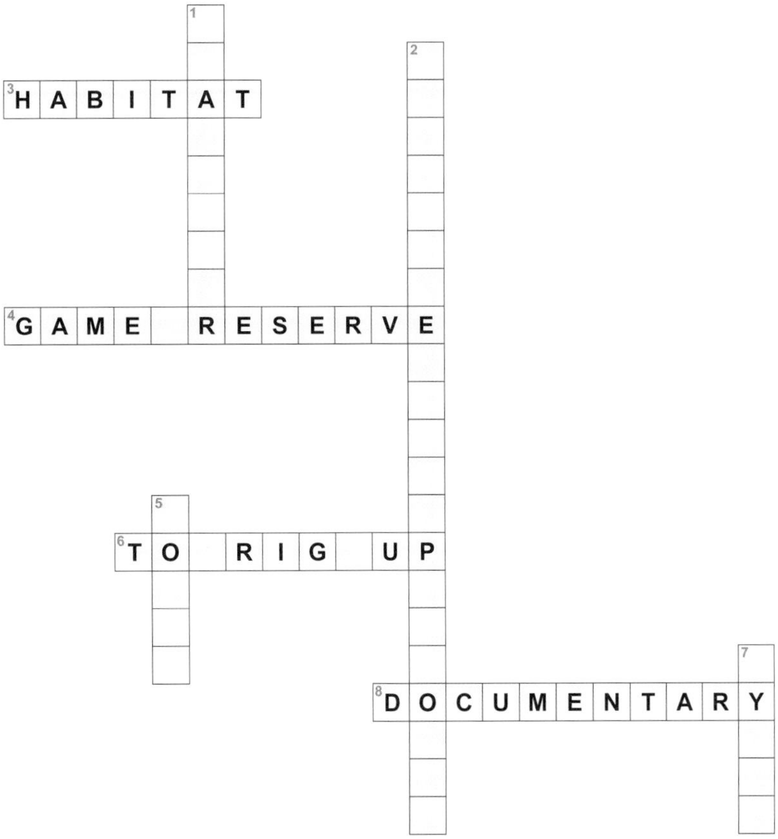

Split-Crossword (student B)

Unit 1

Unit 2

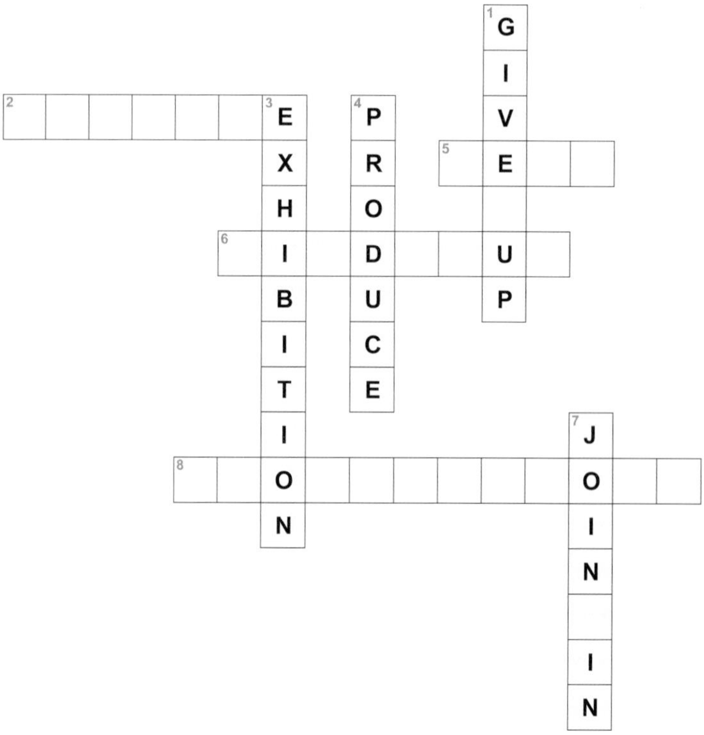

Unit 3

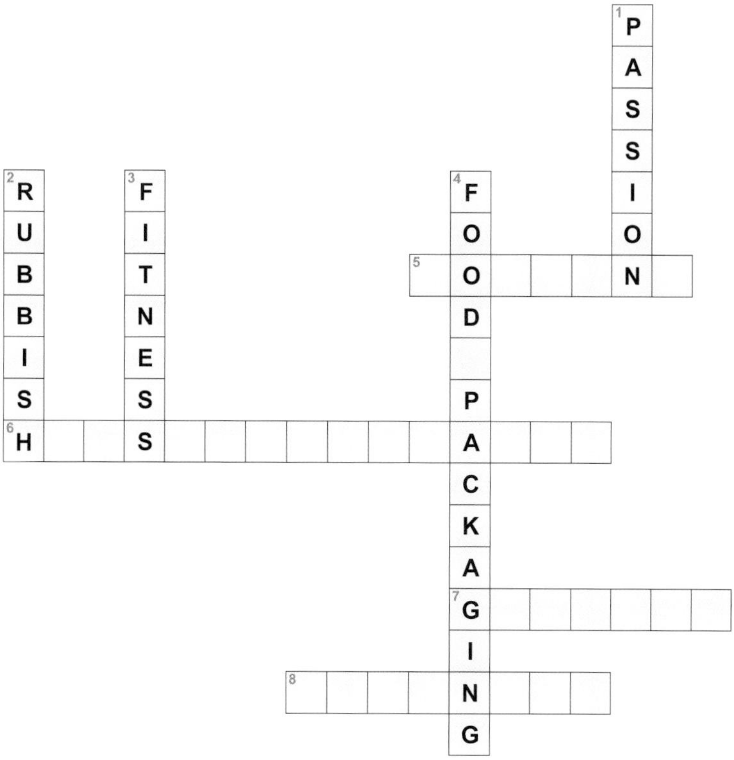
1 PASSION
2 RUBBISH
3 FITNESS
4 FOOD PACKAGING
5
6
7
8

Unit 4

1 GOVERNMENT
2 COMPLETE AGAINST
3
4 ELECTION
5
6 TEENAGER
7
8

Unit 5

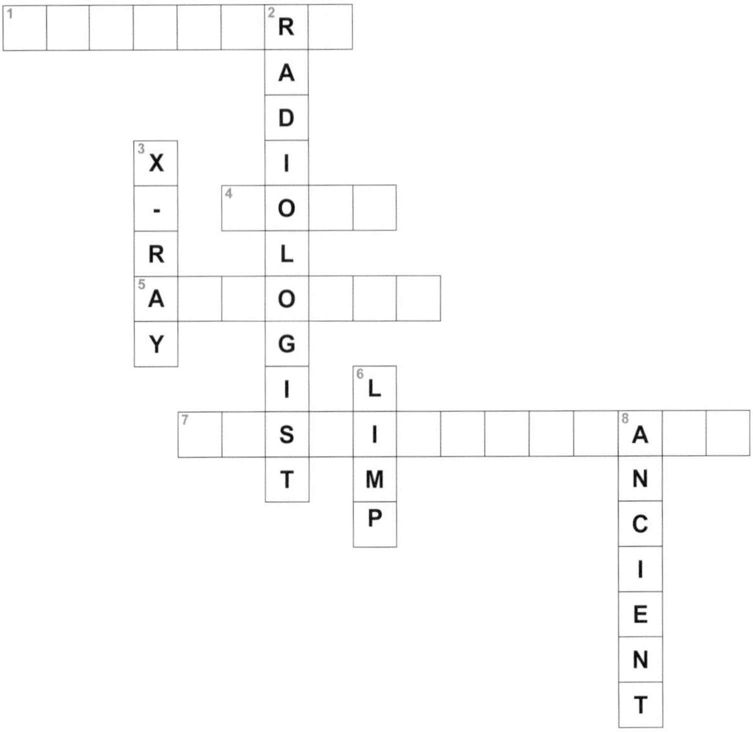
RADIOLOGIST
X-RAY
LIMP
ANCIENT

Unit 6

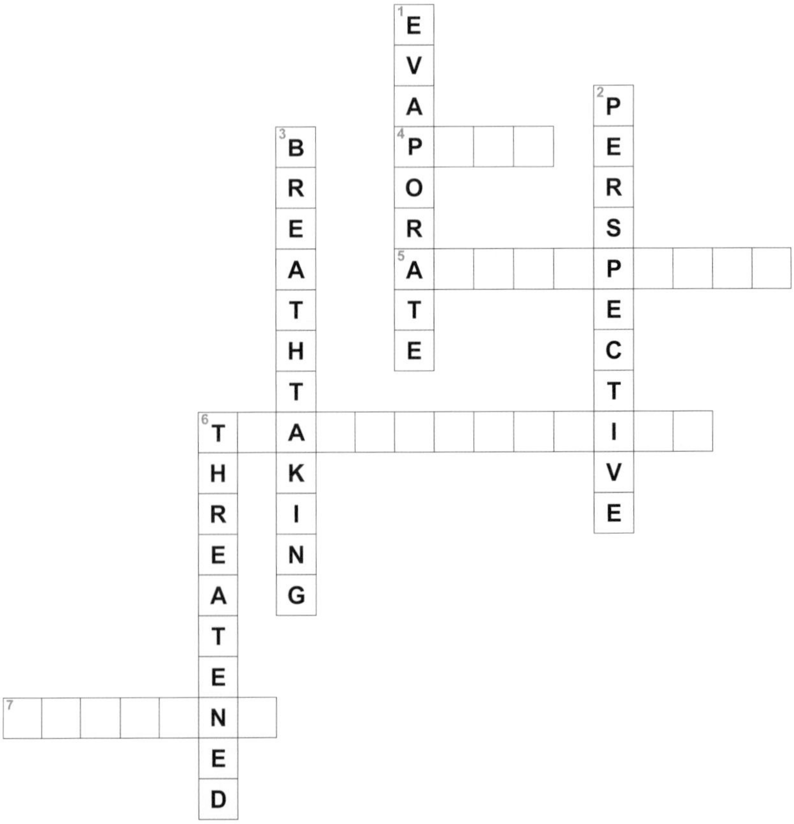
EVAPORATE
PERSPECTIVE
BREATHTAKING
THREATENED

Unit 7

1 S E T O F F
2 E X T R E M E A T H L E T E
3 T O
4 E P I C
5 C R E
6 R I S K
7 L
8 E

Unit 8

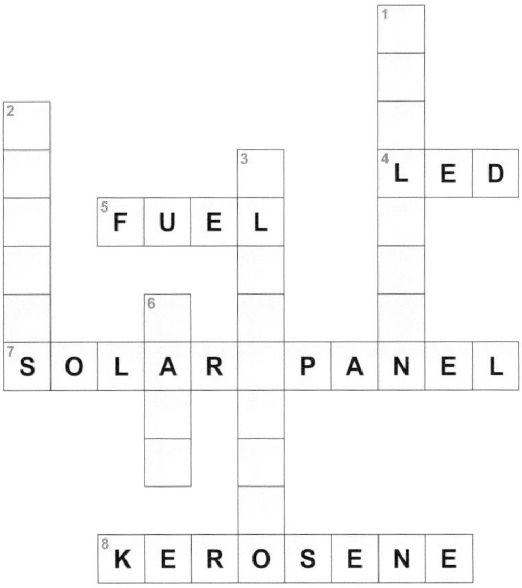
1
2
3
4 L E D
5 F U E L
6
7 S O L A R P A N E L
8 K E R O S E N E

Unit 9

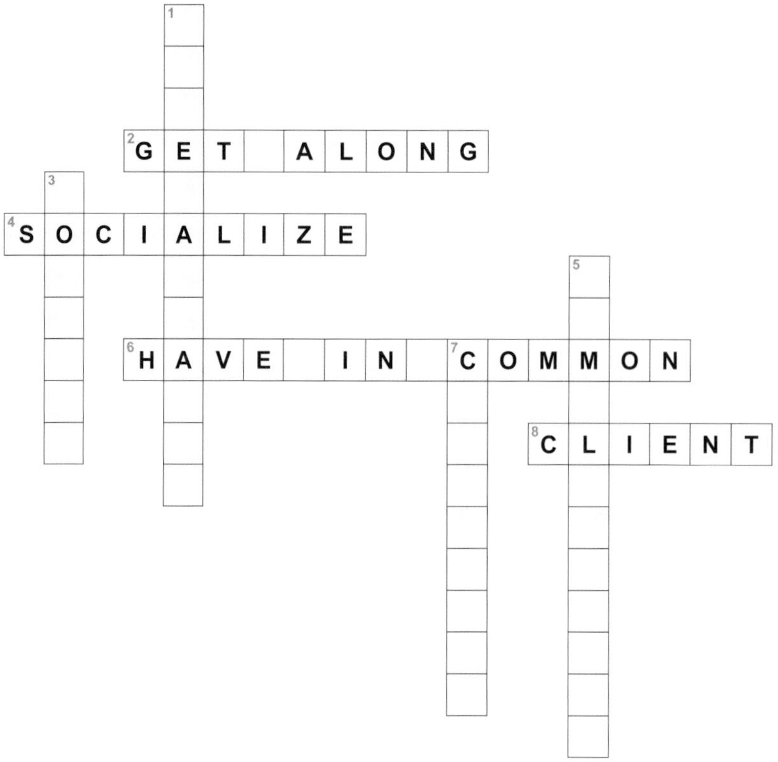

Unit 10

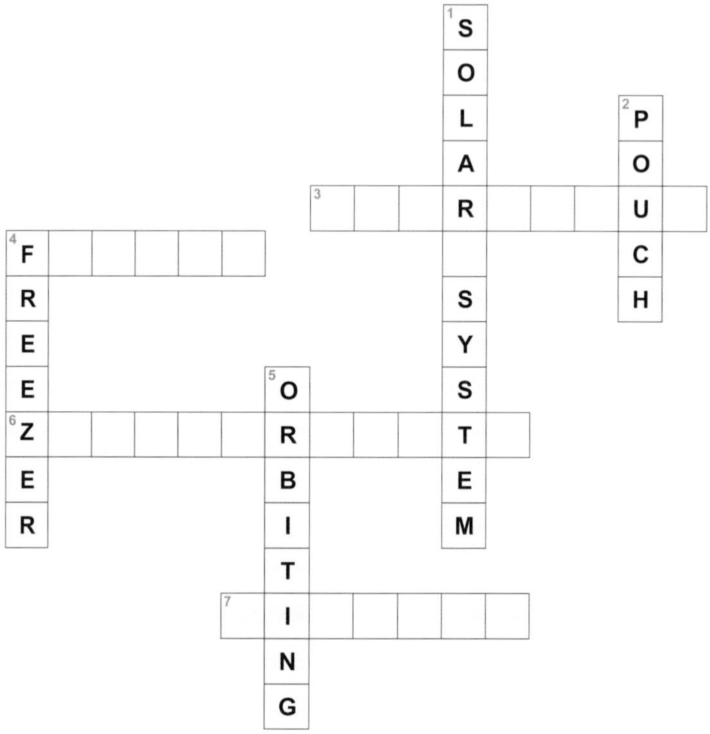

Unit 11

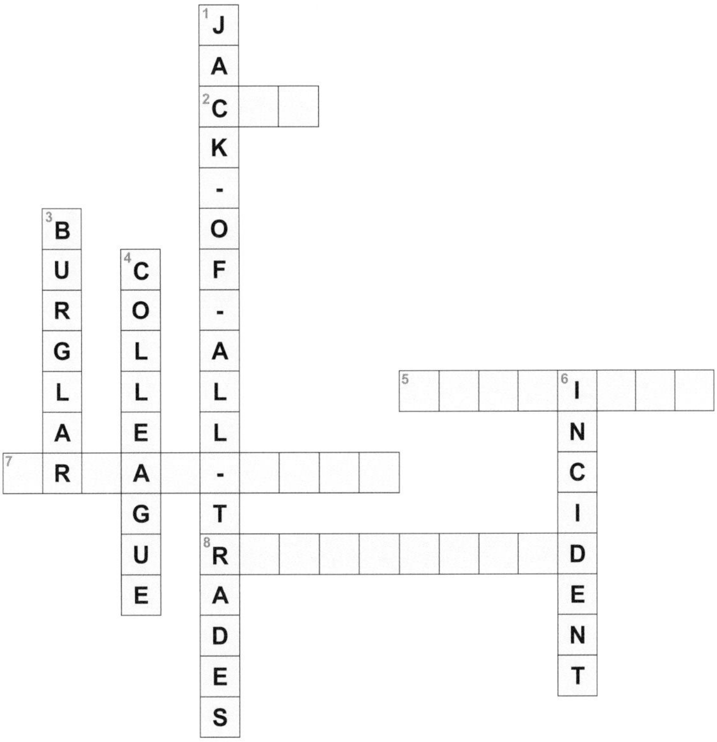

Unit 12

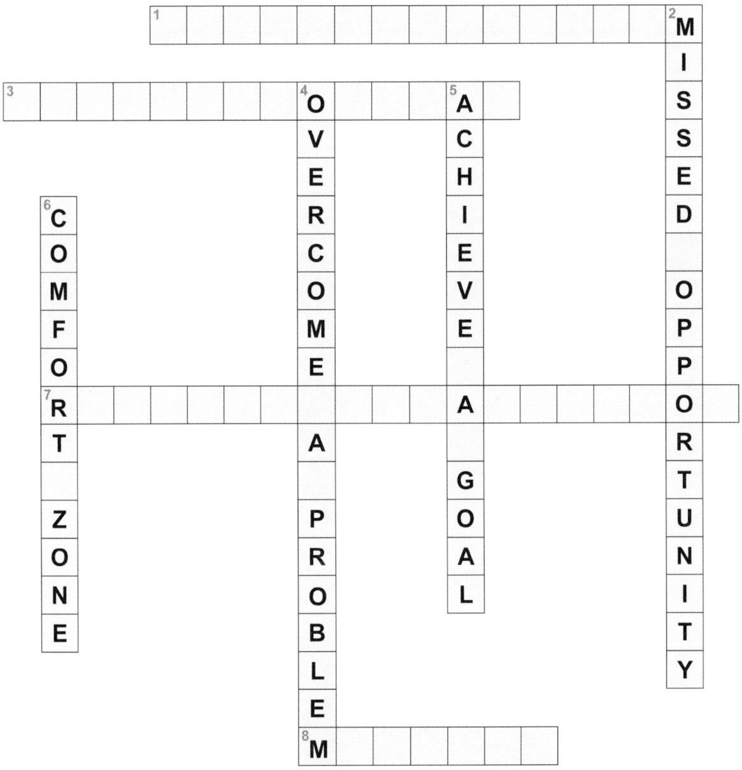

Unit 13

Unit 14

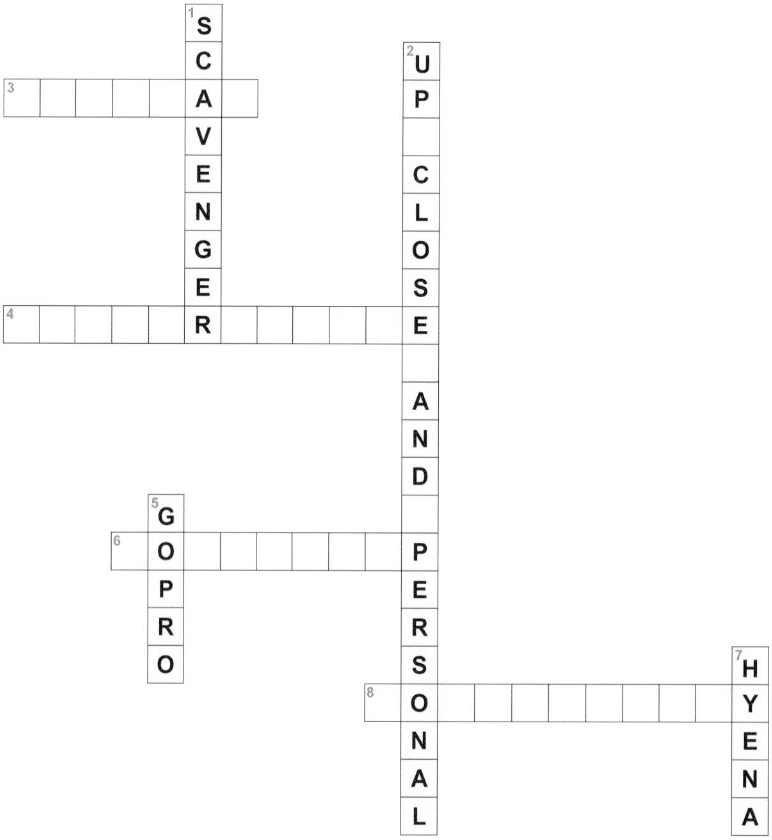

Expanding Horizons: [B-934]
Critical Thinking through Authentic Video〈CEFR B1-B2〉
世界を巡る映像で学ぶ総合英語〈中級〉

1 刷 2022年2月17日
2 刷 2023年8月30日

著 者 チャールズ ブラウン Charles Brown
田邉祐司 Yuji Tanabe

発行者 南雲一範 Kazunori Nagumo
発行所 株式会社 南雲堂
〒162-0801 東京都新宿区山吹町361
NAN'UN-DO Co., Ltd.
361 Yamabuki-cho, Shinjuku-ku, Tokyo 162-0801, Japan
振替口座：00160-0-46863
TEL: 03-3268-2311（営業部：学校関係）
03-3268-2384（営業部：書店関係）
03-3268-2387（編集部）
FAX: 03-3269-2486

編集者 加藤 敦
装 丁 銀月堂
組 版 Office haru
検 印 省 略
コード ISBN978-4-523-17934-4 C0082

Printed in Japan

E-mail nanundo@post.email.ne.jp
URL https://www.nanun-do.co.jp/